Why Did God Create Mosquitos?

Why Did God Create Mosquitos?

A Collection Of 30 Bible-Based Ponderings, Curiosities and Observations

Volume I

Chip Vickio

First Edition

Cabin In The Corner Publishing

30845 Phillips Branch Rd, Millsboro, DE 19966

Contents

Preface

Have you ever had some obscure questions about the Bible? About God? About spiritual things? Questions like, why did God create mosquitos? Or, will there be music in hell?

How about the question, what if Jesus never resurrected? Or, can God's mind be changed? If you're like me, you've got a lot of things to contemplate about God and about the Bible.

I've tried my best to come up with some interesting questions, and to also share some spiritual observations and insights. Some serious. Some with a little humor.

The content of this book is simply a compilation of some of my on-line blog posts. Back in 2012, I decided to start a blog for 2 reasons. First, as an outlet to express my perspectives and Biblical viewpoints as a Christian. And secondly, and more importantly, as a ministry outreach to others. I hoped that it would be encouraging, insightful, and uplifting to readers in showing how awesome our God is.

If you would like to keep up with my latest posts, please visit: **www.chipvickio.blogspot.com**

Chip Vickio 2014

About The Author

Chip Vickio grew up in Watkins Glen, N.Y., and moved near Rehoboth Beach, Delaware, in 1978 with his wife, Francie. They have been there ever since. They have 3 children.

Chip is the Worship Leader at The Crossing, an independent Christian church near Lewes, Delaware. He has led worship there for over 20 years.

He is a Christ Follower, Worship Leader, Musician, Song Writer, Author, Family Man, Bible Teacher, Sky Watcher, and a Lover of Palm Trees and Blue Water.

"But grow in the grace and knowledge of our Lord and Savior Jesus Christ. To him be glory both now and forever! Amen."   - 2 Peter 3:18

CHAPTER 1

Why Did God Create Mosquitos?

I read a headline the other day..."Man's Most Dangerous Insect: The Mosquito". It's true! That disgusting, blood-sucking mosquito! Because of that nasty insect, millions of people have died from the deadly diseases it carries, such as malaria and yellow fever. And people in countries such as Africa are still dying.

We, in America, don't realize what a threat malaria is to people in other parts of the globe. People in Africa can't believe that we don't deal with the terrible disease of widespread malaria here. To them it sounds impossible, unimaginable. They deal with it all the time. But guess what's creeping in right here in the United States? The West Nile Virus. And guess who spreads it? That's right, the deadly mosquito.

When you think about it, the mosquito is a totally disgusting insect. Sucking out your blood!! And who's blood was it sucking before it got to you? That's revolting. And what about the after effects of a single mosquito bite? Not only does this wicked creature suck your blood, its sting causes welts that itch like crazy. And still worse, the possibility of it carrying disease.

To top it off, this insect can fly. And it's aggressive. It's after you! It sneaks up on you. Yuck! I hate these creatures. And if there are a group of people standing around, outdoors, at night, guess who the mosquitos attack first? That's right, me!

When I was in Tanzania, Africa, we slept inside mosquito nets at night. They are made of fine mesh, and placed like a tent over your bed. Even though we were taking anti-malaria drugs, we were still frightened of those lousy insects. Fortunately, for the three weeks we were there, we didn't get bit once! But we were cautious and fearful of them buggers.

So why would God create such an insect? He is the creator of all things, so why? Here's one man's scenario. It's possible that in the Garden of Eden, where everything was peaceful, pleasant, and perfect, the mosquito was not a sick-minded, blood sucking, vampire menace, but a nice, friendly, good-natured, nectar feeding creature. It could be that the sound of it's wings sang out pleasant melodies at night. Maybe in harmony with hundreds of others. OK, maybe that's a little too much.

Then came the fall of man - the sin of Adam and Eve - they ate fruit from the only tree in the garden that they were forbidden by God to eat - the tree of the knowledge of good and evil.

"But you must not eat from the tree of the knowledge of good and evil, for when you eat from it you will certainly die." **(Genesis 2:17)**

When sin and corruption came into the world, everything changed, and went downhill from there. All of creation was affected, not just Adam and Eve. That's when that lousy vermin, the mosquito, first turned on us. And Adam and Eve were their first victims. Can you imagine what they thought when they received their first bite? "What in the world is going on here?"

Not only did the mosquito turn on them, everything seemed to be against them. Because of their sin, all creation was cursed, plants, animals, and humans!

Disease, sickness, pain and death entered the world. Even the ground started to produce thorns and thistles. They never had thorns and thistles before! O, the consequences of sin!

And to the man he (God) said:

"Since you listened to your wife and ate from the tree whose fruit I commanded you not to eat, the ground is cursed because of you. All your life you will struggle to scratch a living from it. It will grow thorns and thistles for you, though you will eat of its grains." (Genesis 3:17-18)

Yup, thorns and thistles started to grow. Thanks a lot, Adam and Eve! And that's not all. Because of their sin, all women from then on will have pain in childbirth, as part of this curse!

To the woman he (God) said:

"I will make your pains in childbearing very severe; with painful labor you will give birth to children. Your desire will be for your husband, and he will rule over you." (Genesis 3:16)

Because sin entered the world, Adam and Eve no longer lived in a perfect world. The tree of life was cut off, and their lives, as well as the lives of all humans to come, would end in death.

By the sweat of your brow you will eat your food until you return to the ground, since from it you were taken; for dust you are and to dust you will return." **(Genesis 3:19)**

Because of the fall of man - the sin of Adam and Eve - when they disobeyed God and ate the forbidden fruit, all Hell broke loose, sort of literally. Satan had accomplished his goal, to influence Adam and Eve, and tempt them into sinning against God, causing all kinds of consequences. And Satan is still at work today.

So, it's not that God created mosquitos to bite, annoy, and kill millions. It's that sin corrupted the world. And because of the influence of Satan, everything is corrupted, including the nasty mosquito. That's the problem....we have corrupt mosquitos! So kill as many of those varmints as you can. It's war! And as for Satan, you'll get yours in the end!

"Against its will, all creation was subjected to God's curse. But with eager hope, the creation looks forward to the day when it will join God's children in glorious freedom from death and decay." **(Romans 8:20-21)**

......and freedom from mosquitos!!!!

CHAPTER 2

The Most Controversial Verse In The Bible

In today's world, there is one verse that stands as the most controversial verse in the entire Bible. It's controversial because in this day and age, people take a strong stand either for or against it. The verse......Genesis 1:1. That's right, the very first verse in the Bible is the most controversial scripture. And yet, it hasn't always been that way. But because of the theory of evolution, which is fairly recent, relatively speaking, this verse is highly contested. That's because Genesis 1:1 claims there is a Creator.

"In the beginning God created the heavens and the earth." (Genesis 1:1)

It's interesting that the very first verse of the Bible sets the tone. This verse is huge in its importance. For those who believe in a Creator God, this verse is foundational and powerful. For those who believe in a Godless evolution, this verse is nonsense and ignorant. That's why each side is so polarized. Take your pick. You can't have both. Notice what the verse says. In the beginning, meaning before time, before the physical realm, before matter existed, God existed. Then God decided to create - the heavens and the earth, including all of life's forms, as shown in the following verses of Genesis chapter one.

"In the beginning GOD CREATED the heavens and the earth." (Genesis 1:1)

Genesis chapter one is diametrically opposed to the philosophy of Godless evolution - that by chance and the combination of the right components, life started in it's tiniest form, then through millions of years, advanced to human life.

In the beginning God created - or - in the beginning random chance started everything. What's your position?

Oh, then there is the idea of Theistic evolution. That's for those non-confrontational people. They like to have it both ways, so there's no arguing. They say, maybe God used evolution to create. That's not only nonsense, it is a cowardly escape route that conflicts with all the Bible truths that tell otherwise. God is never a God who just starts something and stands back and does nothing. Throughout the Old and New Testaments, God always is interactive and intervening. He never abandons us. The idea of Theistic evolution discounts and diminishes God's immense power and abilities, and downplays them as if to say He is not able or capable of creating the entire universe, including life, by His word, in spontaneous fashion.

Another way many try to compromise and reconcile creation and evolution is to explain that everything is made by "intelligent design". Sounds nice, but falls short. It's true, God is the Designer, but much more than that. He not only designed, He created - brought everything into existence.

"Where were you when I laid the earth's foundation? Tell me, if you understand." **(Job 38:4, God speaking).**

"In the beginning GOD CREATED." What's your position? A Creator or not? So many are dissuaded from the truth of a Creator by fine sounding arguments - for example, by TV shows that can sound so convincing. All you need is a well-produced show, with amazing graphics, music, and a persuasive commentator along with impressive sounding credentials, and millions are hooked into falling for it.

"It is I who made the earth and created mankind on it. My own hands stretched out the heavens; I marshaled their starry hosts." (Isaiah 45:12)

"GOD CREATED." To boil it down even further......God or no God? Do you believe in God or not? If not, then all kinds of physical, God-less explanations must be developed, not only for creation, but for all other Biblical miracles. For if God is not Creator, then He is not sovereign over all existing natural and physical laws. But because God is Creator, He can alter the laws of physics and nature, and, for example, split the seas, or walk on water, or instantly heal the paralyzed, or bring someone back from the dead.

"The fool says in his heart, 'There is no God.'" (Psalm 14:1)

In man's attempt to disprove a Creator God, and through human reasoning, explain the unexplainable, namely the origin of matter and the origin of life, all kinds of intricate, outlandish theories are woven. We are bombarded with them. And I'm tired of the propaganda. But don't be persuaded by Godless explanations!

Believe what you may. You know where I stand!

CHAPTER 3

Will There Be Music In Hell?

We know there will be music in Heaven. But will there be music in Hell? I mean, in Heaven, there is a vision given to us in the book of Revelation showing praise and worship around the Throne. There are harps mentioned. There are songs being sung. There is great positive participation. But in Hell? No mention of music. We can just speculate....is it simply the fact that Hell is void of music? Or could it be.....music torture!!!

Think about it. Is there a song that you just can't stand? Is there a song that prompts you to immediately change the channel at the exact moment it comes on? Do you cringe, cover your ears, or even run out of the room when a particular song plays? Could it be, for those who descend to the pits of Hell, that not only is there torture, fire, and torment, but your most hated song continually plays, over and over and over and over. For eternity. Non-stop.

Now, sometimes, if you're like me, when a song you can't stand unexpectedly comes on, you cover your ears and hum. I've got news for you. No humming allowed in Hell.

This is not to say that there is no singing in Hell. Most likely, there is a strong possibility that you will actually be forced to sing your most hated song. That's right, you will be forced to sing the song that disgusts you the most! At the top of your voice. Over and over and over and over. For eternity. Now that's torture!

In Heaven, there are nice, new songs being created all the time.

"And they sang a new song....." (Revelation 5:9).

Everything is fresh and pleasant. But in Hell......no new songs! Just the old ones, over and over again. And I've got news for you. These old songs won't be all your favorite oldies. They will all be a collection of songs that you hate with a passion.

Now in Heaven, beautiful harmonies are sung by massive choirs. But let me ask you this. Have you ever sang next to someone who is actually a worse singer than you? (I know for some of you that's not possible.) Well, in Hell, everyone around you is not just singing your most hated song along with you. They are singing off key as well.

By the way, in Hell, there is actually some background music playing all the time. In Heaven, there's also background music, but it consists of beautiful melodies. On the other hand, in Hell, all the background music, as well as all music there for that matter, is extremely out of tune. If it's one thing that is absolutely annoying, it's listening to an instrument that's out of tune. You guessed it. In Hell, everything is out of tune.

How about the genre of music, the style of music? What music genre do you like the most? Country, Bluegrass, Jazz, Classical, Opera, Rap, etc? Forget it. You won't be hearing any of your favorite stuff in Hell. No. Playing constantly in the background is the style of music you absolutely loathe. And when you hear your most hated songs being sung in the background, guess what? They will be sung by a voice that sounds exactly like whatever particular artist's voice you couldn't stand here on earth (In some cases, it may be sung by the actual artist).

In Heaven, the instruments are beautifully made, and wonderfully played. The harps are probably made of solid gold with precious stones as decorations, and the sound is breathtaking. In Hell, the instruments are junk. Or worse, they are instruments you can't stand to listen to. For me, I can't stand the sound of bagpipes. I'm making extra sure I'm not going to Hell just so I won't have to deal with that! Maybe for you, it's an out of tune violin, or a screeching bugle, or a whatever is most detestable to your ears. Yes, that's what's waiting for you if you end up in the flaming abyss.

One more thing. In Hell, while all these terrible songs are being played or sung, there's an annoying, loud, disruptive sound every 15 seconds or so. Sometimes a horn, or a gong, but most likely a siren. And guess who's behind making these crazy noises? Satan himself! All the while laughing and taunting you.

So, the next time you hear a song starting to play that you really hate, just remember, you're just experiencing a quick glimpse of what Hell will be like! And believe me, you don't want to go there!

CHAPTER 4

Jesus, The Bible, And Basketball

We watch a lot of basketball. The sport is intertwined in our family. I was thinking........just for fun, can basketball be related to Jesus, or at least the Bible? I know what you're thinking....NO! But as I'm sitting in my office (the local Panera's), I'm wondering....could there be some parallels there? And my first conclusion....NO! I mean, I can't visualize Jesus and the disciples playing basketball. Although I guess there's no reason why they couldn't have some occasional fun together - after all they did go fishing together.

After a couple of coffees, and pondering on such a ridiculous scheme, yes, I concluded that there actually could be some similarities (with a little stretching). After all, in basketball, there are players, there are spectators, there are coaches, there are referees, and there's the rulebook. Ahhh...now your getting the picture.

So where does Jesus come in? Here's where....every NBA team has a head coach. He is the overseer, the chief shepherd of the team. He has authority over the team and has the final say. In this parallel of Jesus, the Bible, and Basketball.....Jesus is the Head Coach. He is our:

"Righteous Judge" (2 Timothy 4:8)

"High Priest" (Hebrews 4:14)

"Chief Shepherd "(1 Peter 5:4)

He has all authority (Matthew 28:28), holds the highest place (Philippians 2:9), and in Him, all things hold together (Ephesians 4:16).

A really good NBA coach not only makes good decisions for the team, but loves the game, and loves his players. Jesus loves His church and those that are His. In the same way that any good coach would want to relate to his players, Jesus desires to have a great personal relationship with us.

OK, so everything falls under Jesus. Now what about the Bible? That's easy....the rulebook! In the NBA, there are very specific rules, and they are laid out in great detail, in writing. Without the rulebook, how would the players play? How would the referees officiate? There would be chaos. The NBA rules must be obeyed by the players or there will be turnovers, personal fouls, and even possible ejection from the game. Without the Bible, we would have no guidelines for living, no understanding of how to live the right way, and no way of knowing how to please God and Jesus. (By the way, God the Father is sort of the NBA Commissioner)

We, as Christians, are the players. We need to not only please the coach (Jesus), and be obedient to Him, we need to play this game of life to the best of our ability. We may mess up, even have some personal fouls along the way, but let's keep trying to improve by practicing, by better understanding the rule book, and by listening to the coach. We need to work on our offense (evangelism) and our defense (resisting the opposition).

The NBA referees keep the players in check. When a player does something wrong, the ref points it out. In a similar way, the Holy Spirit convicts us of sin. When we mess up and sin as a Christian, we know it. And as the refs guide the players and are active and present on the court, the Holy Spirit is present and dwells in us, and convicts us.

There are a lot of great plays in basketball. There is the assist, where a player sets up another player to score. Likewise, let's be an encourager to our Christian brothers and sisters, and be a fellow servant. Another play is the pick and roll, where two players work together blocking and passing, just as we should work together in the Kingdom with the common goal of spreading the Good News and ministering to others. And let's not forget the most dramatic and powerful play in basketball, the slam dunk. (Our baptism).

I can't help but think of the crowd - those cheering for their team. A serious fan of a particular team will wear the team's colors, or the team's name on their clothes. They love their team, they root for their team, they cheer for their team, and they support their team. Likewise with Jesus and His Church, we should be worshipers, and we should boast about our team and our coach. We should be enthusiastic. We should cheer for our team. We should support our team, the local church. We should love our team and try to persuade others to do the same. We should become ambassadors for our team (2 Corinthians 5:20).

Wow - I guess there actually are a lot of parallels after all! And I'm sure you can come up with even more on your own. Yes, Jesus, the Bible, and Basketball - they really do have a lot in common!

One more thought. As you play on the team, try to play as hard as you can, and work on developing your skill to the best of your ability. Study the rulebook. Play your heart out for the team and for the coach, and remember that your main goal is to win the game, and not play for your own glory. During the game, you may stumble and foul (sin). But when you do, get up, try not to repeat your mistakes (repent), and go for the win (Heaven). But by all means, be on guard, and make sure you never, ever, get ejected from the game!!!!

:3

CHAPTER 5

A Fortune Teller's Demise

A long, long time ago, I went to a fortune teller. It was probably back in the early seventies. I would never go now. My trust and confidence is now in God alone. Back then, my spiritual maturity was pretty much zilch. I went for fun, sort of on a dare, with a skeptical attitude.

The fortune teller was an elderly lady who lived in an old house on a city street. There was a small sign out front, "Fortune Teller". I don't remember in what city the house was located, but I think maybe Elmira, NY. My wife, Francie, was with me. After being greeted at the door, she agreed to talk with us, brought us into the living room, and charged us a few dollars. Then, one at a time, we met with her, upstairs in a small, plain, empty room with 2 wooden, creaky chairs. There was nothing fancy about the room. It was like a scene out of a haunted house movie.

Francie was first, while I waited downstairs. Then after about 15 minutes, Francie came down the stairs, looking like she'd seen a ghost (just kidding). It was then my turn to talk to the fortune teller, so I made my way up the staircase. I don't remember much of our conversation. She said some general statement about my grandfather that apparently didn't mean much to me since I can't recall it now. However, I distinctly remember one thing she said - that I would come into good fortune and be successful in music, but not until late in life.

Well, here I am in my sixties, and yes, I am incredibly blessed at this stage. Not with much money or wealth, but with a loving family, great friends, and an intimate relationship with God, which gives me contentment, peace, joy, and hope. I've been in a full-time music ministry for the past 11 years that gives me purpose and fulfillment, living my passion, and playing music. I didn't have all this early on. I didn't even care about God until I was in my late thirties. So, yes, as I reflect back, the fortune teller's prediction seems to have come true.

But, there is a warning in all this. Although it may be true that there are some fortune tellers who can actually predict the future, where is their ability coming from? Is it from God, or is it from the dark side? In whom or in what are you putting your trust, your hope, and your confidence? That's the issue. God wants your trust, hope, and confidence in no one or nothing else but Him alone. That's the problem with going to a fortune teller.

God despises divination (the practice of seeking knowledge of the future or the unknown by supernatural means). That's because in God's eyes, it's placing another god before Him. It's turning to some other 'divine' supernatural nature other than Himself. Remember the first of the 10 Commandments:

"I am the Lord your God....you shall have no other gods before me." (Exodus 20:2-3)

God does not like the idea of His people, His children, turning to other sources.

"Let no one be found among you who sacrifices their son or daughter in the fire, who practices divination or sorcery, interprets omens, engages in witchcraft, or casts spells, or who is a medium or spiritist or who consults the dead." (Deuteronomy 18:10-11)

And it's not that the other sources are all fake! There is a spiritual reality which includes the devil. That's what's scary.

An interesting event involving a fortune teller is recorded by Luke, the writer of the Book of Acts. Luke was traveling with the Apostle Paul as they encountered a female slave who had an evil spirit. She was possessed, yet was actually proclaiming truth.

Once when we were going to the place of prayer, we were met by a female slave who had a spirit by which she predicted the future. She earned a great deal of money for her owners by fortune-telling. She followed Paul and the rest of us, shouting, "These men are servants of the Most High God, who are telling you the way to be saved." She kept this up for many days. Finally Paul became so annoyed that he turned around and said to the spirit, "In the name of Jesus Christ I command you to come out of her!" At that moment the spirit left her. (Acts 16:16-18)

It seems that this incident of a demon possessed person speaking truth about Paul and his fellow workers was something that really annoyed Paul. It just didn't seem right. There seemed to be deception involved. She was speaking what seemed like good news alright, following them around for days, but perhaps her motives were wrong. One thing is for sure - she was gaining credibility for herself, which she could use for evil purposes later.

This section of scripture really got me almost laughing out loud. I could just see Paul getting more and more fed up with her until finally enough was enough. Alright already!! At first she may have seemed harmless, but after a while, she became obnoxious. Maybe I think it's funny because sometimes I can relate to what Paul was feeling when I deal with certain people. And I think you can too. Paul became so aggravated that he turned around and performed a miracle, casting out the evil spirit from the possessed woman. Thus ending her career, to her demise. And her owners weren't too happy with Paul either, as you can see in the rest of chapter 16. But, hey!! Think about this....it was this slave girl's demise as a fortune teller, but it was her release into freedom from being in bondage by an evil spirit! I like to think that she took heed of Paul's message after that incident, and became a believer and follower of Christ.

So I guess the lesson is this.....there are such people as fortune tellers even in today's world. Some are fake, but some may be real. Regardless, stay away from them. If they are real, what source are they tapping into? Certainly not God since He teaches against trusting and confiding in such people. Instead, put all your hope, all your faith, all your confidence in Almighty God, and in Him alone.

"May the God of hope fill you with all joy and peace as you trust in him, so that you may overflow with hope by the power of the Holy Spirit." (Romans 15:13)

CHAPTER 6

My Euphemism Nightmare!

My wife and I and a group of friends had just finished hearing a sermon that warned us about the use of euphemisms. The topic was fresh on all of our minds as we arrived at a friend's house to play cards. A euphemism is a word that is used as a less offensive substitute for an objectionable word. The preacher implied that we all have developed a bad habit of using euphemisms as substitutes for blasphemous words.

He suggested that this was not acceptable because our intent was still the same. Therefore, in a religious context, his conclusion was that we were still guilty. For example, instead of using the Lord's name in vain, such as the exclamation, "O my God", or blurting out "Jesus Christ", we substitute a euphemism such as, "O my Goodness", or "Jiminy Cricket". Instead of saying damn, we say darn.

Was our good intention of substituting certain words for 'bad' words acceptable with the Man above? As our card game got underway, we mulled over the question of our guilt in the use of euphemisms. And as time went on, all of us began to be more critical of how we substituted words.

On the first round of cards, my wife got a bad hand and quickly shouted, "O sugar!". Immediately, we pointed at her and found her guilty of a euphemitical error. We knew that she really meant was, "O sh__".

With each hand we began to spew out more and more euphemisms, and each time a person said one, the others would point at the accused and find them guilty on the spot. On one round of cards, someone exclaimed, "Son of a gun". We all pointed and yelled. We knew what they meant. The next round someone got a good hand but said, "Holy cow". Again, we all pointed and jeered. The more we played, and the more intense the game got, the more we became accursed. "Gosh darn it". "Jeepers".

After a while it seemed like it was safer to say nothing, but the card game kept us off track through the excitement and challenge of the game. The euphemism accusations continued until we couldn't seem to draw a line between an acute case and a mild case, or as the Catholics might say, a mortal euphemism and a venial euphemism. This started to accelerate when I was dealt three aces and innocently said softly, "wow". Everyone pointed at me and yelled, "Euphemizer!"

After a while, things escalated to the point where it seemed that no one knew when to draw the line. Was any form of exclamation a euphemism? Even someone's "whew" drew wrath. A cough was questioned. Clearing of the throat was out. After a while I started guarding my language to avoid any chance of a euphemism. Could I possibly make it through the game without any more accusations? The game was not of cards anymore but was a challenge to see who could complete the game without saying any more euphemisms.

I was determined to make it through. However, to my demise, it didn't take long until I made a fatal error. During the last deal, I couldn't help being excited over what was certainly the winning hand. In a sense of confidence and pride, I slightly raised my right eyebrow. O No! I immediately realized what I had done, but it was too late. I had been spotted, and accused of yet another euphemism. Guilty, I was utterly defeated. Thanks preacher! I hope I don't go to heck because of all of this!

CHAPTER 7

The 1-2 Punch To Overcome Worry

OK - I know - we're not supposed to worry. But as humans, we all tend to do it. I think it's one of our most negative inherent traits. So, why is it so bad to worry? One reason is that it produces nothing but anxiety and stress. And more often than not, the things we worry about either never happen or they simply work themselves out. Because of that, worry is usually a waste of time, as we go on and on, tormenting ourselves with worst-case-scenarios. Not only will constant worry drive you crazy, it can actually be detrimental to your health. Simply put, worry doesn't do us any good.

"Can any one of you by worrying add a single hour to your life?" **(the words of Jesus, Matthew 6:27)**

Perhaps the strongest case against worry is that it is diametrically opposed to our faith and trust in God. That's why Jesus seemed disgusted when the disciples were afraid they were going to die because of the storm on the sea, even though Jesus was with them.

He replied, "You of little faith, why are you so afraid?" Then he got up and rebuked the winds and the waves, and it was completely calm. **(Matthew 8:26)**

I'm not saying it's easy to stop worrying. As for myself, I don't know if I can completely overcome it. But lately, I've discovered a way to reduce it, and I want to share this plan with you. It works for me, and perhaps it will help you too, in trying to take steps to conquer worry.

Lately, my worries have been about my children. Naturally, as a dad, I'm concerned about their well being. At one point they were all scattered around the world. My son, daughter-in-law, and my grandson in Africa, my youngest daughter in Australia, Western Europe, Africa, and the Philippines, and my other daughter and her husband in Tennessee (I never knew Tennessee was so close to Delaware where I live).

I've caught myself worrying about their health, safety, provision, etc. However, over time, I've found a one-two punch combination that has really helped me to the point that I've found some peace of mind. Here it is:

The One-Two Punch To Overcome Worry

1. Pray Specific Requests

First, whatever it is that is worrying you, pray specifically to God about it. Ask God for His providence, His intervention, His hand to work in your favor. For whatever specific situation you are concerned about, ask for the outcome that you desire. In this way, you are casting all your anxiety on Him, for Him to handle, allowing Him to take control. After all, that's what He wants us to do.

"Cast all your anxiety on him because he cares for you." **(1 Peter 5:7)**

2. Then Pray "The Prayer of Trust"

Once you pray a specific prayer, then follow up with what I call "The Prayer Of Trust". I came up with this prayer after realizing that in my worry, I was not turning my concerns over to God, not trusting in Him. I was just leaving things to happen by chance. I realized that worry was a weakness, perhaps a weakness in my faith in God! Once I began admitting this, and praying this prayer, I felt peace. Here is "The Prayer Of Trust". Feel free to quote it and take it as your own.

The Prayer of Trust: "Lord, please forgive my tendency to worry, and help me to take this worry that I have and replace it with Trust in You."

It's all about transforming worry energy into trust energy. And that's done with God's help, through prayer. The next time worry pops up, and it will, the quicker you fight it, the better. Remember the combo: Specific Prayer + Trust. This one-two combination may not be a knock-out punch, but it certainly will do some heavy damage in the battle against worry. God does not want us being anxious about anything. Instead, He wants us to give it all to Him, let Him handle it, and trust Him with the outcome. His desire for us is to have peace, not fear and worry. And that is so comforting to know.

"Do not be anxious about anything, but in every situation, by prayer and petition, with thanksgiving, present your requests to God. And the peace of God, which transcends all understanding, will guard your hearts and your minds in Christ Jesus." **(Philippians 4:4-6)**

CHAPTER 8

The Ransom Of Captain Charlie Spade

The story of Captain Charlie Spade is similar to what happened to Captain Richard Phillips, the ship captain who was taken hostage by the Somali pirates in 2009 in the Indian Ocean, off the dreaded northeast African coast.

Picture this... the Estonia Emperor, with Charlie Spade at the helm. A 950 foot cargo container ship, cruising in the dark of night off the coast of Somalia, Africa. Things were going fine until they made a foolish mistake. They tried to make better time by taking a shorter route that brought them dangerously close to the shoreline, a practice that the shipping company prohibited. Nonetheless, Captain Charlie Spade and his crew took their chances, thought they could get away with it, and gambled that in the dark of night, while at full speed, they could avoid any possible pirate attack.

Sure enough, the worst case scenario unfolded. A small blip showed up on the radar, closing in fast. Armed pirates were chasing them down with the intent to board the ship, take the crew as hostages, and hold the ship until a large ransom was paid. Captain Spade tried to outrun them, but the huge vessel could only max out at about 28 knots. That's about 32 mph, no match for the pirate speed boat.

The pirates reached the ship in no time. The crew had been alerted and was ready to try some evasive tactics such as turning on high power water canons which blasted water from the top of the ship toward the surface of the sea. However, the pirates were able to maneuver around that, and successfully throw hook and ladders to the side deck. Unlike the crew of the Estonia Emperor, who had no weapons on board, the pirates were heavily armed with machine guns, grenade launchers, and rifles. The crew had no recourse but surrender with their hands up as soon as the pirates spotted them.

The pirates ordered Charlie to slowly bring the ship in close to the shore, anchor it, and wait for a ransom to be paid for the release of the ship as well as the crew. They were in trouble, not only because they were being held hostage, but also because they disobeyed company policy. The shipping company ended up paying a very large ransom...7 million dollars. After receiving the payment, the pirates released the ship and its crew, and they were set free. And even after discovering his illegal route, the shipping company reconciled their relationship with Captain Charlie Spade, and he continued to serve as a captain, convinced to never disregard any shipping company policy ever again.

The story of Charlie Spade is an illustration of Biblical redemption. Charlie's disobedience got him in trouble, similar to how our sinful nature, early on in our lives, gets us in trouble. Charlie was held hostage. Similarly, we are held hostage by sin which can entangle us, shackle us, take us captive, and separate us from God.

There's no way Charlie was going to be released by the pirates unless either force was taken or a ransom was paid. The definition of a ransom is this....."money that is paid in order to free someone who has been captured or kidnapped". In a sense, we are captured or kidnapped by sin, become separated from God, and there's no way to be released from sin except by God's own doing.

The shipping company paid the high ransom price which freed Charlie Spade. Likewise, God paid our ransom price - the price to free us from the bondage of sin. It cost God a lot. This payment that freed Charlie redeemed him. To redeem is essentially to 'buy back' or better yet, to 'trade for payment', like redeeming a coupon at a department store. That coupon is as good as money.

Regarding the ship, the captain, and the crew, the shipping company said to the pirates, "They are mine!" And the company was willing to pay the price. Regarding us, as sinners, God says, "You are mine!" And He is willing to pay the price.

God must see every person as extremely valuable, even when it may seem that we are undeserving, unworthy, and sinful. That's proven by the astronomical price that He is willing to pay. The price God is willing to pay is the life of His one and only Son. But we must accept God's offer of the 'payment'. That's done through faith and obedience in Christ, committing our life to Him as our Redeemer, Savior, and Lord. If we accept the offer, Jesus trades His life for ours! The sacrifice of Jesus redeems us, frees us, forgives us, and reconciles us with God.

We all sin and fall short of the glory of God. It's true of every human. Still, because of His love and His grace, God's payment of ransom, through Jesus, is available to anyone. And just as Charlie Spade needed to be rescued, and just as his relationship with the shipping company needed to be reconciled, we can be rescued, and our relationship with God can be reconciled. Have you accepted God's offer to be redeemed, to be bought back? If so, walk faithfully. If you haven't yet, will you accept His offer to pay your ransom?

"For you know that God paid a ransom to save you from the empty life you inherited from your ancestors. And it was not paid with mere gold or silver, which lose

their value. It was the precious blood of Christ, the sinless, spotless Lamb of God. God chose him as your ransom long before the world began, but now in these last days he has been revealed for your sake. Through Christ you have come to trust in God. And you have placed your faith and hope in God because he raised Christ from the dead and gave him great glory. You were cleansed from your sins when you obeyed the truth, so now you must show sincere love to each other as brothers and sisters. Love each other deeply with all your heart. For you have been born again, but not to a life that will quickly end. Your new life will last forever because it comes from the eternal, living word of God." (1 Peter 1:18-23)

CHAPTER 9

The Man Who Astonished Jesus

I'm sure Jesus experienced all kinds of people while He was on earth. People who surprised Him. People who disappointed Him. People who even made Him angry. But there's a particular man who astonished Him - in a good way!

You see, Jesus, while He was on earth, was specifically looking for something. He was searching intensely. He was always on the lookout for it. Everywhere He went, and every moment He was awake, He was searching and searching, trying to pick it up on His radar screen. And unfortunately, most of the time, it wasn't there. Time after time, He was disappointed. Yet, He kept on anxiously looking.

Before I tell you what it is that Jesus was so earnestly desiring to find, let me introduce to you the man who had it. Jesus was well into His ministry when He met a Gentile man, an unlikely one to have what Jesus was looking for. That's because you would think that Jesus would find it among the Jews, His people, the chosen people. But no, it was a Gentile man, a non-Jew.

This Gentile man was a military commander in the Roman army. This, however, was not what impressed Jesus. And it wasn't that he was a man of authority. That didn't impress Him either. What astonished Jesus was what this Gentile man possessed....great faith! That's right, Jesus was astonished by the degree of faith he had. That's because Jesus had not found anyone in Israel, not anyone among what was supposedly God's people, who had such great faith as this man! This Gentile commander, called a centurion, absolutely believed that Jesus had the power of God, and that Jesus was able to do all things. Here's how the story goes:

When Jesus had entered Capernaum, a centurion came to him, asking for help. "Lord," he said, "my servant lies at home paralyzed, suffering terribly." Jesus said to him, "Shall I come and heal him?" The centurion replied, "Lord, I do not deserve to have you come under my roof. But just say the word, and my servant will be healed. For I myself am a man under authority, with soldiers under me. I tell this one, 'Go,' and he goes; and that one, 'Come,' and he comes. I say to my servant, 'Do this,' and he does it." When Jesus heard this, he was amazed and said to those following him, "Truly I tell you, I have not found anyone in Israel with such great faith. (Matthew 8:5-10)

There are at least 4 things that must have certainly impressed Jesus about the centurion.

1. He was a Gentile but still believed in Jesus, regardless.

Of all people, it was a Gentile who turned out to have great faith! Impressive. Jesus was a Jew, and came into the world as the long awaited Jewish Messiah, but as a whole, was rejected by His own people. So for a Gentile to have such great faith was amazing. He may not have understood that Jesus was God in the flesh, but he knew that Jesus was an authentic man of God, regardless if he was a Jew or a Gentile.

2. He was humble.

The centurion could have been one prideful person considering the position he held. Yet, he displayed humility. He obviously regarded the authority and sovereignty of Jesus as much greater than his. He told Jesus that he did not deserve to have Him come to his house. This statement reveals that he was underserving of the miracle he was asking for. He was totally relying on the Lord's grace, and was at the mercy of Jesus.

3. He was a compassionate man

The centurion was so sincerely concerned about his servant, that he didn't just send a messenger to Jesus, but he personally went to plead with Jesus himself. It shows his love and compassion for those around him, including his servant. And he was relying on the love and compassion of Jesus for healing.

4. He was absolutely confident that Jesus could do it.

The centurion knew all about authority, and all about giving commands. He believed Jesus, without a doubt, had the power to heal. Not only that, the centurion was so sure Jesus had the power to heal, he believed all Jesus had to do was say the word, from a distance, and his servant would be healed immediately without even Jesus being at the house where the servant was. And that's exactly what happened!

"Then Jesus said to the centurion, 'Go! Let it be done just as you believed it would.' And his servant was healed at that moment." (Matthew 8:13)

The centurion, in the eyes of Jesus, had great faith. Jesus, while on earth, was always looking for great faith. Unfortunately, He was disappointed time and again. Remember when Jesus calmed the sea, and the disciples were scared that they were going to die?

"He replied, 'You of little faith, why are you so afraid?' Then he got up and rebuked the winds and the waves, and it was completely calm." **(Matthew 8:26)**

Or the time Jesus walked on water, and Peter began to go to Him but took his eyes off Jesus?

"Immediately Jesus reached out his hand and caught him. 'You of little faith,' he said, 'why did you doubt?'" **(Matthew 14:31)**

There are many more examples of doubt and lack of faith, however, that doesn't mean there were not any examples of people who did have faith. There were many. As a matter of fact, Jesus even performed several healing miracles as a response to a person's faith. There's one other example of 'great faith' besides the centurion, and it's by a Canaanite woman in Matthew 15, a Gentile! (The 2 examples of 'great faith' were by Gentiles, not Jews!)

Jesus was always looking for faith when He was on earth. But it doesn't stop there. Jesus asked a question that should rock you:

"....when the Son of Man comes, will he find faith on the earth?" **(The words of Jesus in Luke 18:8b)**

Jesus is still looking, even today, and until He comes back, for people who have faith. I suppose the real question is whether or not He sees faith in you and I. Even if we start with faith a small as a mustard seed, it can grow if we water it.

He is always searching, looking for those who have faith, hoping to find it. Will He?

"So then faith comes by hearing, and hearing by the word of God." (Romans 10:17)

CHAPTER 10

The Type Of Music God Hates!

According to the Bible, there's definitely a certain type of music God hates! Did you think I was going to say Rock and Roll? No, I'm not talking about Rock! Especially since that's the music I used to play. Is it Country or Bluegrass? Not that either. How about Rap? Hip-hop? Jazz? Would you guess Classical? Pop? Maybe Heavy Metal? Soul? Rhythm and Blues? Reggae? Blues? No, none of those either. I'm not talking about a certain genre.

And I'm not talking about the idea of God hating a particular song. Can you picture that? God covering His ears when a song that He can't stand is played? Ha, I doubt that too (well, maybe, considering some of the songs that have been written). As for me, there are a couple of songs that drive me crazy. One is the old song, "The Lion Sleeps Tonight" and the other, "Who Let The Dogs Out". But, I'm not talking about God hating a certain song.

And I'm not talking about God hating the music played by a particular musical instrument being used. Although, there are some instruments that man has invented that are very irritating. The one I can't bear to listen to is the bagpipe. To my ears, a bagpipe is always dissonant and out of tune. I wonder if God hates a certain instrument that man has come up with? There are all kinds of musical instruments mentioned in the Bible - such as lyres, harps, flutes, horns, trumpets, tambourines, and cymbals. Nothing to indicate He dislikes any. But as far as the type of music God hates, I'm not talking about an instrument.

The type of music God hates has nothing to do with the style of music, or the song's melody, or the song's instruments. The type of music God hates is music that is intended to worship and glorify Him, but is played or sung with a hypocritical heart. He cannot stand it!

In the Old Testament, there was a time when the nation of Israel was corrupt with injustice. The wealthy took advantage of the poor. Extortion and bribery in the court system ran rampant. God was not pleased with them, and as long as this went on, He was not going to bless them. He used the prophet Amos to give the Israelites the message that repentance is the only way to avoid destruction. And as far as the nation's hypocritical religious gatherings and songs of praise, this is what God said:

"I hate all your show and pretense—the hypocrisy of your religious festivals and solemn assemblies I will not accept your burnt offerings and grain offerings. I won't even notice all your choice peace offerings. Away with your noisy hymns of praise! I will not listen to the music of your harps. Instead, I want to see a mighty flood of justice, an endless river of righteous living." (Amos 5:21-24)

Because these people's lives weren't right with God, He called their worship songs "noisy hymns of praise!" And God refused to listen to the music of their harps. He hated it and called it "noise".

I just wonder, if we are singing songs of worship and praise, and we don't really mean what we say, or we are hypocritical in what we sing, does God feel the same way toward us? Yikes! I would say yes! If we are playing or singing music, and we are just going through the motions with false motives or hypocritical hearts, forget it! God refuses to hear it. Not only that, He hates it!

And if we are living a sinful lifestyle, and then pretending to be worshiping God on Sunday, or any other day, it won't work. God is looking at our hearts, and we should be worshiping from our hearts. Otherwise our efforts are in vain. God will not accept or hear our songs of praise and worship. But if we are trying to live righteous lives, are in Christ and under His grace, then we can lift our songs to Him with thankful hearts, and He will accept them.

"Sing psalms and hymns and spiritual songs to God with thankful hearts." (Colossians 3:16b)

One more thing. As far as God listening to our music, I think there are three basic categories of songs: songs He is pleased with, songs He is neutral to, or songs He hates.

1. Songs God is pleased with.

These are songs that glorify and honor Him. WIth these, He is pleased and listens, when they are presented with a sincere heart.

2. Songs God is neutral to.

These are secular songs and include all genres and all instruments. With these I believe He is neutral.

3. Songs God hates.

These are songs that are hypocritical. He hates these, as well as any songs that deny Him or are offensive to Him.

So, let's make sure our worship is real and our hearts are true.

"But the hour is coming, and now is, when the true worshipers will worship the Father in spirit and truth; for the Father is seeking such to worship Him. God is Spirit, and those who worship Him must worship in spirit and truth." (John 4:23-24)

CHAPTER 11

Snake On A Pole

I really am fascinated by the amazing parallels in the Bible between the Old and New Testaments. There are so many examples of people, places, events, or things in the Old Testament that are fulfilled in the New Testament.

There is a term for this called typology. The word is a little confusing. Think of an old manual type writer that uses hammers for each of the individual letters. When a key is pressed, a hammer strikes the paper, making a slight indentation in the paper along with the ink. Likewise, certain Old Testament persons, places, things, events, etc. are sort of a faint impressions or models of what is more clearly brought to light in the New Testament. For example, the story of Jonah (three days in the whale) is just a faint imprint of what is greater to come - Jesus three days in the grave.

I wanted to give this introduction because many of my future posts will be on such typology topics, although some of the comparisons I make may not be true 'typology' in a purest sense, but rather what I like to call 'amazing parallels' of the Bible.

Now, to the story of a "snake on a pole". This is an example of Biblical typology. This story starts in the Old Testament and ends in the New Testament. In the Old Testament, there is a scene described where the nation of Israel is grumbling and complaining. After all God had done for them through Moses - led them out of Egyptian slavery - miraculously gave them food (manna) - and protected them - there was a time when the people of

Israel started to complain as they were traveling in the wilderness. They began to speak against God and Moses.

"Why have you brought us out of Egypt to die here in the wilderness? There is nothing to eat here and nothing to drink. And we hate this horrible manna!" (Numbers 21:4-5).

Wrong thing to do! Because they spoke against Him and against Moses, God decided to punish them severely. He sent poisonous snakes among them. Some Bible translations call them fiery serpents. Fiery serpents sure sounds more terrifying. Maybe they were called fiery because of the inflammation resulting from the bites, or maybe because of the judgment against them by God (many times fire signifies judgment in the Bible). Regardless, these serpents began biting the people, and many died. Then the people realized what was going on and came to Moses, crying out.

"We have sinned by speaking against the Lord and against you. Pray that the Lord will take away the snakes." So Moses prayed for the people. (Numbers 21:6-7).

God heard Moses' prayer and through His mercy, God decided to provide a way out for them - a way of rescuing them - a way of healing them. Now He could of just done that through a clean sweep sort of miracle. But He instructed Moses to do something very strange - probably something that didn't make much sense at the time.

God told Moses to make a replica of a poisonous snake and attach it to a pole. He told Moses all who are bitten will live if they simply look at it! So that's exactly what Moses did. He made a bronze snake and put it up on a pole. And sure enough, when anyone was bitten by a poisonous snake and they looked at the bronze snake, they lived! (Numbers 21:8-9). Which means that if someone got bitten and didn't look at the bronze snake, they would die. This cure was conditional, it was their choice to stare at the snake on a pole and trust that it would cure them, and it did!

Now the story could have just stopped there and it would have been an incredible story. As a matter of fact, it did stop there for a long, long time - until the Apostle John reflected on it. John realized something - that this whole serpent on a pole thing had double importance. First, it was obviously a miracle of healing, saving the people. But secondly, and more importantly, it was a prefigure, a model, of Jesus crucified on a cross! Maybe that's why God came up with this snake on a pole idea to begin with.

One of the most popular verses in the Bible is:

"For God so loved the world that he gave his one and only Son, that whoever believes in him shall not perish but have eternal life." (John 3:16)

But take a look at the two verses that lead up to it - John 3:14-15. That's where John compares the story of the snake on a pole to belief in Jesus!

Just as Moses lifted up the snake in the desert, so the Son of Man must be lifted up, that everyone who believes in him may have eternal life. For God so loved the world that he gave his one and only Son, that whoever believes in him shall not perish but have eternal life." (John 3:14-16).

There are several parallels that John is making. First, just as the poisonous snakes bit the people, sin poisons us. Second, just as the people would die if they didn't look at the snake, believing that it would cure them, we will die in our sins if we don't believe in Jesus, who offers us life. Third, just as the snake was lifted up on a pole, Jesus was lifted up on a cross, for our sake. Fourth, just as the bronze snake was the one and only cure for the people, Jesus is the one and only cure for the sins of all people. Fifth, just as the people needed only to look at the bronze snake, we are saved, not by good works or deeds, but by grace.

I'm sure you could come up with even more parallels in this story. What's important to remember though, is that this comparison of the Old Testament bronze snake story to Jesus on the cross is a legitimate comparison because the Apostle John teaches it as such.

So from now on, when you hear the story of the snake on a pole, let it remind you of Jesus and how he saves you. And may your eyes continue to look toward Him, for healing and for forgiveness.

"Let us fix our eyes on Jesus, the author and perfecter of our faith, who for the joy set before him endured the cross, scorning its shame, and sat down at the right hand of the throne of God." (Hebrews 12:2)

One more interesting thing.....the Bible mentions the snake on a pole in one other place. It occurs in 2 Kings

18:4. It's when King Hezekiah smashes it to pieces, hundreds of years later. By that time, it had become an object of idol worship. Perhaps they trusted the snake for healing instead of trusting in God Himself. King Hezekiah wanted to do right in the sight of God, so he got rid of all the false idols, smashed the sacred stones and cut down the Asherah poles.

"He broke into pieces the bronze snake Moses had made, for up to that time the Israelites had been burning incense to it." (2 Kings 18:4).

It makes you wonder, would we do the same today if we had a piece of the actual cross, or the ark of the covenant, or a part of Noah's ark? Would we worship those things more than God Himself? (Romans 1:25). Maybe there's a good reason we don't have such things.

CHAPTER 12

Marriage Advice From A 100yr Old Woman!

In March, 2013, we celebrated my Mom's 100th birthday! At the time, she lived in the southern tier of New York State with her younger sister, who was 98 at the time!.

When we were visiting my Mom for her birthday celebration, I got several chances to capture on video many conversations that we had. She talked about memories of childhood and of her teenage years, about her philosophies on today's world, about her view on faith and prayer, and we talked about many other topics as well.

In one of the videos, I asked her, "What is your advice on marriage?" I was really interested in what she had to say. And I thought that her answer would be a good one to hear since she was such a devoted wife to my Dad for about 40 years. After he died, she would never entertain even just the thought of being with another husband. She was definitely a one-man woman, and that was final.

When I asked for her advice on marriage, I didn't give her any advance warning, or any time to prepare. Perhaps that was a bit unfair, not giving her a chance to get her thoughts together, but it was interesting to hear her candid, off-the-cuff response. She talked slowly, like she was carefully trying to craft the words to use in her answer.

So here is her advice on marriage, word for word, taken directly from the video.....

She said, "Let me think...that's a hard one! First, to be true to each other...not to keep secrets or things from each other. Communication is very important. And to pull for one another, and think about the other more than yourself. If you think about the other more than yourself, you'll be happy, because that way, the other partner, in turn, will do it for you. He will return that love, faithfulness and sharing. And most of all, if you have God in your life - if you live without some sort of religion in your life, it's hard to make it. You've got to have God! If you turn God away, you don't find peace. If you see a lot of divorced people, or unhappy people, quarreling, you'll notice....they've shut God out of their life. They don't go to church. They don't have anything to keep them together."

I really liked her advice - how not to keep secrets from each other, and the fact that communication is so important. That's so true! And how about the Biblical principal she used....to put the other first. It reminds me of the following verse:

"Do nothing out of selfish ambition or vain conceit. Rather, in humility value others above yourselves, not looking to your own interests but each of you to the interests of the others." (Philippians 2:3-4)

I liked her statement that we should "pull for one another". In other words, we are never to criticize or put down the other person, either to their face or behind their back. Instead, we need to be our spouse's greatest encourager. That, in itself, is priceless advice when you really think about it!

"...encourage one another and build each other up..." (1 Thessalonians 5:11)

She used a three word phrase that really describes a good marriage, "love, faithfulness, and sharing". Well said, Mom! When you see a marriage with those three attributes, you can be sure it's a healthy marriage. When love, faithfulness, and sharing are consistently happening on both sides, the relationship is strong.

"Love is patient, love is kind. It does not envy, it does not boast, it is not proud. It does not dishonor others, it is not self-seeking, it is not easily angered, it keeps no record of wrongs. Love does not delight in evil but rejoices with the truth. It always protects, always trusts, always hopes, always perseveres. Love never fails..." (1 Corinthians 13:4-8)

Finally, she states her most important foundational principle that has guided her whole life.....that God is foremost. She sees this as the key in holding marriages together - that both spouses must have a faithful, trusting relationship with God. She is a devoted, faithful, life-long Christian herself - a believer in Jesus - a Christ follower. When she said, "You've got to have God!", she said it ever so emphatically, with a very concerned look on her face, like she was questioning how it would even be possible not to have the Lord in your life and still have a marriage filled with joy and peace.

I, myself, have found it true, not only in my marriage, but in so many people's lives around me - that without the Lord in your life, everything will tend to fall apart. As the scripture says:

"He is before all things, and in him all things hold together." (Colossians 1:17)

I'm so proud of my Mom. I respect everything she says, all of her wisdom, as well as her ongoing example to all of us. Sometimes my Mom will say, "I don't know why the Lord let's me live so long." I know the answer!.....It's because she has been a blessing and a wonderful example to so many people. Especially to me.

CHAPTER 13

The Day The Earth Stood Still

Warning....to some, this chapter will seem to have some outlandish claims. It may stretch your belief system a bit. But first, you must really ground yourself on the following concept:

"For nothing is impossible with God." (Luke 1:37).

After all, God is Creator! And if God is Creator, that means that He not only oversees everything, but He can intervene in the physical realm at any time, and even defy what we would call the laws of physics or science. I like the word 'defy'. To defy is - to challenge to do something considered impossible. A miracle, for instance, is basically defying the laws of nature. Miracles are considered impossible as far as science is concerned. Walking on water is impossible. Calming the raging sea is impossible. Bringing back a dead person to life is impossible. But, of course, as far as God is concerned, "nothing is impossible."

The other concept you must be convinced of is this:

"the entire universe was formed at God's command, that what we now see did not come from anything that can be seen." (Hebrews 11:3)

This statement is incredible. It means that God is so powerful that He created everything, including the entire universe, just by His command - "the entire universe was formed at God's command." Wow! Consider this:

"The Lord merely spoke, and the heavens were created. He breathed the word, and all the stars were born." (Psalm 33:6).

Not only that, He created everything from nothing. In other words, he created 'matter' itself, instantaneously. He didn't just make everything out of pre-existing matter - He made matter itself! But again, remember,"nothing is impossible with God."

A God so powerful is able to do anything, on any scale, large or small. The Creator is more powerful than what He has created, and is sovereign over what He has created. That means He can, at any time He chooses, alter or change what He has put in place. If He is powerful enough to put something in place, He is certainly powerful enough to alter it. Do you believe it?

That brings us to the incomprehensible: the day the earth stood still. That's right, a day when the earth stopped rotating for a day! Seems 'impossible' doesn't it? The earth rotates at just over 1000 miles per hour! It's impossible to stop this rotation - or is it? Scientists will say it's impossible. But don't listen - believe instead. Scientists will say life is created by evolution, not creation. Scientists will say there couldn't have been a world flood that covered the earth. Scientists will say that the star of Bethlehem was a natural event.

I like what God says about those who proclaim to know things that are not meant to be comprehended by man.

"Where were you when I laid the foundations of the earth? Tell me, if you know so much. Who determined its dimensions and stretched out the surveying line? What supports its foundation, and who laid its cornerstone as the morning stars sang together and all the angels shouted for joy?" (Job 38:4-7).

God continues to put Job, as well as any human, in his place. Being facetious, He says:

"Where does light come from, and where does darkness go? Can you take each to its home? Do you know how to get there? But of course you know all this! For you were born before it was all created, and you are so very experienced!" (Job 38:19-21)

Yes, the earth stopped in it's tracks. It's recorded in the book of Joshua.

"On the day the Lord gave the Israelites victory over the Amorites, Joshua prayed to the Lord in front of all the people of Israel. He said, "Let the sun stand still over Gibeon, and the moon over the valley of Aijalon." So the sun stood still and the moon stayed in place until the nation of Israel had defeated its enemies. Is this event not recorded in The Book of Jashar? The sun stayed in the middle of the sky, and it did not set as on a normal day. There has never been a day like this one before or since, when the Lord answered such a prayer. Surely the Lord fought for Israel that day!" (Joshua 10:12-14)

You see, God stopped the rotation of the earth so that the sun could stand still, giving them extended light for battle.

But there's even a more incredible miracle! There was a time when God not only stopped the rotation of the earth, but moved it slightly backwards for a moment, before allowing it to rotate again.

Meanwhile, Hezekiah had said to Isaiah, "What sign will the Lord give to prove that he will heal me and that I will go to the Temple of the Lord three days from now?" Isaiah replied, "This is the sign from the Lord to prove that he will do as he promised. Would you like the shadow on the sundial to go forward ten steps or backward ten steps?" "The shadow always moves forward," Hezekiah replied, "so that would be easy. Make it go ten steps backward instead." So Isaiah the prophet asked the Lord to do this, and he caused the shadow to move ten steps backward on the sundial of Ahaz! (2 Kings 20:8-11)

So....believe what you may. As for me, nothing is impossible with God. I believe He stopped the earth's rotation twice. If you believe in the Creator God, who are you to put limits on Him? Who are you to tell him what He can and cannot do? What gives you the authority to question these things? - or dare to tell God He didn't or couldn't do such things?

And if God can do such incredible things like stopping the earth's rotation, imagine what He can do in your life.

"Now all glory to God, who is able, through his mighty power at work within us, to accomplish

infinitely more than we might ask or think." (Ephesians 3:20).

CHAPTER 14

The Wise Men - How It Really Went Down

If you know me, then you know the typical manger scenes you find on Christmas cards, or even in Church yard displays, drive me crazy. It's because they usually are not scripturally accurate. They often portray the wise men at the manger. Sometimes they show a star or angels over the manger. These are far from true. I understand they are trying to cram all the components of the birth of Jesus into one setting, just don't base your theology on a Hallmark greeting card or on some church's manger scene! Check out the scriptures for yourself - Mathew chapters 1 and 2, and Luke chapters 1 and 2.

Regarding the Wise Men, below is my version of their timeline. You may not agree with me in every detail, but that's ok, as long as your opinion is Bible based.

THE TIMELINE

Scene 1: Near Bethlehem, during the night that Jesus was born, shepherds tending to their sheep in the fields were startled when "suddenly an angel of the Lord appeared among them, and the radiance of the Lord's glory surrounded them. They were terrified!" (Luke 2:9). It's important to note the term "the radiance of the Lord's glory". This should not be down-played or overlooked. It was an extreme, miraculous illumination and must have been very powerful. If it was 'of the Lord's glory', it must have been incredibly bright. The angel announced to the shepherds that a Savior was born that same day in a manger in Bethlehem. Look what happens next:

"Suddenly a great company of the heavenly host appeared with the angel, praising God.." (Luke 2:13).

I doubt that this great company of the heavenly host appeared in the dark. On the contrary, they must have appeared in this spotlight called the 'radiance of the Lord's glory'. Some translations call the great company of the heavenly host a multitude, or a vast, heavenly army. To totally illuminate this vast, heavenly army, the radiance of brilliant light must have extended up into the heavens, with an enormous diameter - sort of a pillar of light. And you thought lasers were powerful! Such an array of brilliance in the night time sky would have been visible for miles - possibly hundreds of miles. No one knows how long it lasted, but at some point, the angels vanished, went back to heaven, and the darkness quickly returned. The scene in the field reverted back to what it was before: the shepherds in the fields around Bethlehem on a quiet, still, dark night. After such an amazing experience, the shepherds did what they never do - they left their sheep in the fields and quickly ran off - to find Jesus.

Scene 2: The Wise Men (also referred to as Magi), probably located in far away Babylon, saw this very same miraculous illumination off in the distance on that particular night. Perhaps hundreds of people from many different locations saw it in the night time sky before it went out. However, the Wise Men reacted to it. They knew it was supernatural - that this was a sign of something of huge importance. It's possible that they were familiar with ancient prophecies, such as recorded in Isaiah and Numbers, that dealt with a coming star or bright light. Regardless, the Wise Men, who were experts regarding the stars, concluded that this supernatural beam of light was in the direction of distant Jerusalem, and that it must have signified the birth of a powerful and important new King of the Jews. Because of this celestial phenomena, they were convinced that it was a once in a lifetime event, and they must make a journey to make homage to this newly born King. Based on the location and direction of this strange light they had seen in the sky, which was no longer visible, they prepared to head to Jerusalem, where they assumed had been the focal point of the light - where this new King must be. It would take a lot of preparation. They would need to get a caravan together, which included supplies, food, animals, and people. Their journey could take weeks or even months.

Scene 3: While the Wise Men were just beginning their journey, baby Jesus was brought into Jerusalem from Bethlehem. After Mary's days of purification (ceremonially unclean from delivering a baby boy) were over, forty days as defined by the Law ((Leviticus 12:1-8), Mary and Joseph brought Jesus into the Temple, right under Herod's nose. She was to go in front of a priest to offer a sacrifice. Because she offered a sacrifice that was representative of those who were poor (Luke 2:24), it confirms that Wise Men had not arrived yet with their valuable riches which included gold.

Scene 4: The Wise Men are well into their journey to Jerusalem. By this time, Mary, Joseph, and Jesus were back in Bethlehem, living in a house. Finally, the Wise Men arrive in Jerusalem. Not knowing where this new-born King was, they did the most logical thing - ask the current king, Herod, for details. Of course, Herod pretended to go along with the Wise Men, but inwardly, he was furious. After all, he was the king and no one was going to take his throne. He summoned the chief priests and the scribes for answers regarding the location of Jesus. The chief priests and scribes were Jews who knew the Old Testament scriptures well, and based on Micah 5:2, they knew the Messiah was to be born in Bethlehem. So Herod sent the Wise Men on their way to Bethlehem, but not before asking them the exact date that they had seen this "star" they had told him about. It was so he could calculate how old Jesus was, assuming the Wise Men saw the 'star' on the night Jesus was born.

Scene 5: As the Wise Men headed toward Bethlehem, something fantastic happened: another miraculous event. The supernatural light appeared again to the Wise Men. They were overjoyed! It had been a long time since they saw the brilliant sign in the sky on the night Jesus was born. This time, they knew that this light was a guiding beacon for them - that would lead them not just to Bethlehem, but the the exact house where Jesus was staying (Matthew 2:11).

Scene 6: The Wise Men entered the house, bowed down before Jesus, and worshiped Him. Then, they presented Him with gifts - gifts that were fitting for a King. Their mission was accomplished. Their quest to find the newly born King was over.

Scene 7: Divinely warned in a dream that they should not return to Herod, the Wise Men departed for their own country another way. Likewise, during that very night, Joseph was also warned in a dream to take Jesus and His mother, flee to Egypt for safety, and stay there until further notice. So Joseph, Mary and Jesus quickly took off during the night before Herod could decide on a plan, and before his thugs could take action, because they probably followed behind and saw the house where the Wise Men entered.

Because Herod realized that he had been outwitted by the Magi, and that by now he was unsure where Jesus was, he was furious. He gave orders to kill all the boys in Bethlehem and its vicinity who were two years old and under, in accordance with the time he had learned from the Magi, hoping to have a wide enough margin to include Jesus in the process (by now Jesus could have been several months, possibly even a year old). A terrible slaughter occurred, but Joseph, Mary and Jesus safely made it to Egypt, where they lived until Herod died. Through God's providence, the valuable gifts from the Magi were God's provision to provide travel and living expenses for Joseph, Mary and Jesus.

CHAPTER 15

Astronomy, Astrology, and The Bible

I remember when I first began coming across facts about astronomy in the Bible. It was and still is amazing - how the Bible confirms science. Or should I say, science confirms the Bible. When you look at passages that describe the heavens, the stars, the moon, the sun and the earth itself, written long before telescopes were invented, it awakens you to the fact that God is Designer/Creator, and His revelations about the universe are found in scripture.

Many people who lived in the days of Columbus believed the earth was flat. Obviously, they never read the Bible! The prophet Isaiah, who lived approximately 700 years before Christ, describes a round earth.

"He sits enthroned above the circle of the earth..." (Isaiah 40:22)

The book of Job is considered by most scholars to be the oldest book in the Bible, and yet it implies gravitational forces!

"He spreads out the northern skies over empty space; he suspends the earth over nothing." (Job 26:7)

Even evaporation is described in the Book of Job!

"He draws up the drops of water, which distill as rain to the streams." (Job 36:27) Wow! *"He wraps up the waters in his clouds, yet the clouds do not burst under their weight."* (Job 26:8)

Here's a good question for you when you look up into the heavens on a starry night.

"Lift your eyes and look to the heavens: Who created all these?" (Job 40:26)

Who created all these? Of course, the answer is God.

"It is I who made the earth and created mankind upon it. My own hands stretched out the heavens; I marshaled their starry hosts." (Isaiah 45: 12)

There are some things we simply can't comprehend. Like, where does the universe end? And if it ends, what's on the other side? And maybe there's a reason why we are not able to understand it all. Maybe such mysteries are God's way of demonstrating that His knowledge is far greater than ours.

"As the heavens are higher than the earth, so are my ways higher than your ways and my thoughts than your thoughts." (Isaiah 55:9)

And we can try with all our might to theorize and speculate how the earth was formed, but to the scientists who leave God out of the picture when it comes to answering the question of how the earth was made, God may very well be saying to them:

"Where were you when I laid the earth's foundation? Tell me, if you understand. Who marked off its dimensions? Surely you know! (Job 38:4-5a)

Ha. I love it when God is being sarcastic! And when He asks rhetorical questions like the one above. The answers to those questions are certainly obvious.

The prophet Jeremiah lays out the facts perfectly in the next verse.

"He made the earth by his power; he founded the world by his wisdom and stretched out the heavens by his understanding." (Jeremiah 51:15)

While astronomy is the science of the universe, astrology, on the other hand, is the practice of tracking the position of celestial bodies with the belief that they influence earthly occurrences and human affairs. Astrology is interesting because it's tied to astronomy, but there is a problem with it. God doesn't like it! And He doesn't like us to use it, especially if we use it as our life's guide.

Are you one of those who can't wait to get the morning paper, or the internet, to see what you daily horoscope says? Maybe you plan your day, or your week, around it. If so, you might want to rethink this practice. God is a jealous God in the sense that He wants your complete trust and faith in Him, and in Him alone.

"You shall not make for yourself an image in the form of anything in heaven above or on the earth beneath or in the waters below. You shall not bow down to them or worship them for I, the Lord your God, am a jealous God." (Exodus 20:4-5a...one of the Ten Commandments)

God has made it clear that we should be loyal to Him exclusively, and turn to nothing or no one else.

"And do not let your people practice fortune-telling, or use sorcery, or interpret omens, or engage in witchcraft, or cast spells, or function as mediums or psychics, or call forth the spirits of the dead. Anyone who does these things is detestable to the Lord." (Deuteronomy 18:10b-12a)

Do the planets and their alignment influence us? Maybe. Does a full moon affect man's behavior. It sure seems like it! You see the question is not about whether all these things are real or not. The question is this: "In whom or in what are you placing your trust?" That is exactly what God is asking you!

We can look at the heavens with awe and wonder because the universe is fascinating and incredible. But as far as the stars and planets are concerned, we are warned.

"And when you look up into the sky and see the sun, moon, and stars—all the forces of heaven—don't be seduced into worshiping them." (Deuteronomy 4:19a)

Over the centuries, mankind has fell to this temptation of looking to the stars and planets as the controlling force in one's life. This distracts tremendously from God Himself.

"They traded the truth about God for a lie. So they worshiped and served the things God created instead of the Creator himself, who is worthy of eternal praise! Amen." (Romans 1:25)

The prophet Isaiah didn't think much highly of astrologers either.

"All the counsel you have received has only worn you out! Let your astrologers come forward, those stargazers who make predictions month by month, let them save you from what is coming upon you." (Isaiah 47:13)

The bottom line is this.....God wants your trust and faith in Him only. Forget relying on fortune tellers, astrologers, and psychics, or anything else for life's answers. Just rely on Him. That's where our faith should be placed.

And as far as astronomy is concerned, if you are looking to the stars to reveal something to you, let it reveal this.......His glory!

"The heavens declare the glory of God; the skies proclaim the work of his hands." (Psalm 19:1)

CHAPTER 16

Merry Christmas..I Mean "Happy Holidays"

It seams to get worse and worse every Christmas. No one seems to dare to say "Merry Christmas" in public. But listen all you bank tellers, grocery store workers, retail store clerks.....I know you secretly want to say "Merry Christmas!" to your customers. But whatever you do, bite your tongue. You know the company policy. We don't want to offend anyone. Just politely say "Happy Holidays". And don't forget to smile.

Can you imagine what it would do to the company's reputation if you slipped up and said "Merry Christmas"? The customer may throw a fit, storm out, never to return. Or possibly, the customer may actually threaten you. Worse yet, the company could be sued, and by your goof up, the entire business could go under.

How dare you remind someone that the reason for all the December excitement and celebration is.....shhhh (Christmas). Soon even Santa will start exclaiming, "Merry Holiday to all, and to all a good night." Lowes will be selling Holiday trees and Holiday wreathes. And what about the Holiday lights that everyone will put up. Parades will be referred to as Holiday parades. Office parties will be Holiday parties. People will be rushing to buy Holiday presents before it's Holiday eve. And on Holiday day, we can all gather the family to open our Holiday gifts and then later have Holiday dinner together, with Holiday cheer and Holiday candy.

And what about the Holiday songs. They need to be changed too. Soon radio stations will be playing "I'm Dreaming Of A White Holiday", "O Holiday Tree, O Holiday

Tree", "The 12 Days Of Holiday", "We Wish You A Merry Holiday", and they'll dub Elvis' voice to sing, "I'll Have A Blue Holiday Without You".

Christmas (ooops, I mean Holiday) movies will need to be re-released as "White Holiday", "The Grinch Who Stole Holiday", "Holiday Story", and "Holiday Vacation". And what about the great poem, "The Night Before Holiday"? We will need to re-learn everything! "Merry Christmas" will need to go 'underground'!

Somewhere, though, a remnant will remain. There will still be a select few, scattered among us. who secretly will say "Merry Christmas" to each other, maybe softly, maybe even just mouthing the words, silently. But somehow, someway, this phrase, which is on its way to being banned for public use, will survive. There will be a remnant that carries on. And someday children will be taught how long ago, a cheerful, joyous greeting was once exchanged between 2 people at Christmas time, with a smile and a sparkle of excitement in their eyes.

And hopefully, this winter Holiday greeting will eventually come full circle - once everyone realizes who the offended ones really are. WE ARE! It's the Christians! "Happy Holidays" is the offensive term, not "Merry Christmas!" To us, "Happy Holidays!" tries to cover up the real meaning of Christmas. Christmas is all about Christ. If you don't like "Merry Christmas" - sorry! But Christmas is about Christ - and it's about us - Christians.

The reason we say "Merry Christmas!" is because Christ's love is for all people, regardless of who they are. And because of that, we as Christians extend our best wishes to everyone, regardless if you are a Christian or not. "Merry Christmas!"is a positive, gracious, cheerful greeting, not an offensive one.

We need to not be ashamed of "Merry Christmas!", it would be like being ashamed of the Gospel message - the good news of the birth of a baby King, Immanuel, God with us, the King of all kings, who became our King - who brings hope and peace and joy. Now that's something to celebrate, proclaim, and share!

CHAPTER 17

Can God's Mind Be Changed?

Can we alter what God has planned? If God decides to go ahead and do something, can we make Him stop? If the answer is yes, then it would imply that that we, as humans, as mortal creatures, as small as a grain of sand relatively speaking, have the power to change the mind of the Almighty, All-Powerful God! Could this be possible? Isn't there a so called "destiny" that is laid out for us? Or do we have a part to play in how our journey through life unfolds?

First of all, is there any documentation that this idea, changing the mind of God, has ever happened throughout history? Well....let's stop with all the questions, and start looking for answers! Actually, there is documentation! Changing the mind of God has happened, and therefore can happen even now!

Let's look at the story of Jonah. God sent Jonah, the prophet, to warn the people of Nineveh that God planned to destroy their city because of their wickedness. Jonah relayed God's message to the people of the city, "Forty more days and Nineveh will be overthrown." That was God's plan, and the city would have been wiped out, but something changed God's mind and altered the destiny of the people of Nineveh! The reaction of the king and all the people caused God to rethink His plan.

"The Ninevites believed God. A fast was proclaimed, and all of them, from the greatest to the least, put on sackcloth. When Jonah's warning reached the king of

Nineveh, he rose from his throne, took off his royal robes, covered himself with sackcloth and sat down in the dust." (Jonah 3:5-6)

The Bible describes that even the animals were made to fast - not permitted to eat or drink anything. Not only that, the animals were also dressed in sackcloth (a coarse, black cloth made from goat's hair that was worn together with the burnt ashes of wood as a sign of mourning for personal and national disaster; as a sign of repentance; and as a sincere request for deliverance)!

Here is the result of their obvious, sincere actions:

"When God saw what they did and how they turned from their evil ways, he relented and did not bring on them the destruction he had threatened." (Jonah 3:10)

Amazing! They changed God's mind! And it was done by their actions, by their repentance. Because the nation turned from their evil ways, God showed mercy toward them and backed away from His original plan.

Another example of a man altering God's plans is documented in the book of Genesis. Here, in Genesis chapter 18, we find God ready to destroy the cities of Sodom and Gomorrah because of their sin and corruption.

Then Abraham approached him and said:

"Will you sweep away the righteous with the wicked? What if there are fifty righteous people in the city? Will you really sweep it away and not spare the

place for the sake of the fifty righteous people in it?" (Genesis 18:24)

Notice how God responded.

The Lord said, "If I find fifty righteous people in the city of Sodom, I will spare the whole place for their sake." (Genesis 18:26)

What's amazing here is how Abraham negotiates with God! Abraham knew how corrupt the city was, but he also knew his nephew, Lot, lived there with his wife and two daughters. So, he tires to get God to change His mind about destroying everyone in Sodom, and spare the city instead, if only 50 righteous people are found. God agrees.

But even more amazing, Abraham continues to negotiate (knowing that there are probably not even 50 righteous people in the whole city). He convinces God to agree to spare the city if only 45 righteous people are found, then 40, then 30, then 20, then 10. Wow! Of course, as the story goes, not even 10 people could be found righteous, so God destroyed the cities of Sodom and Gomorrah anyway, but not before Lot and his family were rescued.

God was definitely influenced by Abraham's requests, and that's more confirmation that God's mind can be changed, or at least influenced. Because of Abraham's persistent pleas, God showed Him grace and gave in.

So in the above two examples, both mercy and grace are displayed by God. And both are His response to man's interaction with Him. And that's the key. We can actually interact with God! Perhaps the best and most powerful way is through prayer.

Here's the point....God interacts with us in real time. You could say He is a "real-time" God. He is relational. He listens to us and intervenes when He chooses to. He has an open ear, and we have the privilege of making our requests to Him.

And what's really comforting is the fact that whatever our requests are, God will at least consider them. And if He considers our payers, that means He will do what's best for us in the long run as far as how He answers them, or if He answers them, or when He answers them.

So keep on asking, keep on praying, and know that God is listening. And you never know, through His mercy and grace, you may convince Him to take action!

CHAPTER 18

What If Jesus Never Resurrected?

Those who opposed Jesus believed His talk of resurrection from the dead was an absolute hoax. When Jesus died, they were convinced of one thing - His dead body would be still in the tomb after three days. This popular Jesus movement would then die out fast. They had only one concern. His followers might fake His resurrection by stealing the body! That would be big trouble for them.

So....PLAN 'A'.... seal the tomb and place guards there. The chief priests and Pharisees convinced Pilate to do just that. (Matthew 27:62-66)

Nice try, guys. But no match for the spiritual realm, for the supernatural, the power of God! The guards didn't do so well, and on the third day after Jesus died, here's what happened.......HE RESURRECTED FROM THE DEAD!!

"There was a violent earthquake, for an angel of the Lord came down from heaven and, going to the tomb, rolled back the stone and sat on it. His appearance was like lightning, and his clothes were white as snow. The guards were so afraid of him that they shook and became like dead men." **(Matthew 28:2-4)**

JESUS 1 - CHIEF PRIESTS 0

After that episode, the chief priests were in a panic. Now what? If the news got out about the disappearance of

83

Jesus' body from the tomb, it would spark a resurgence of the movement.

So...PLAN 'B'.....Lie! That's right...lie. Bribe the soldiers to spread a fake story that the disciples snuck into the tomb and stole the body. Then maybe that would squelch the movement.

When the chief priests had met with the elders and devised a plan, they gave the soldiers a large sum of money, telling them, "You are to say, 'His disciples came during the night and stole him away while we were asleep.' If this report gets to the governor, we will satisfy him and keep you out of trouble." So the soldiers took the money and did as they were instructed...." (Matthew 28:12-15)

Of course, that backfired. The soldiers could lie about the body of Jesus being stolen from the tomb, but that would only work until either the body was found, or Jesus was actually seen alive. And guess what? JESUS WAS SEEN ALIVE! And not just on one occasion or by one person. He was seen on several occasions by several persons. He even appeared to over 500 at one time (1 Corinthians 15:6).

JESUS 2 - CHIEF PRIESTS 0

Think about it. if Jesus never resurrected from the dead.........

1. We would not have a Savior

If Jesus was still in the tomb, then Christianity wouldn't exist today. His prophecy, "after three days I will rise again", would be in error. Jesus would not be who He claimed to be, and we would still be waiting for a Messiah.

2. We would not have real faith

If Jesus did not come back to life, we would be worshiping a false Lord. Our faith would be useless.

"And if Christ has not been raised, your faith is futile; you are still in your sins." **(I Corinthians 15:17).**

3. We would not have forgiveness

The same verse above states that if Jesus never resurrected, then His death on the cross is futile also. In other words, if He didn't resurrect, our sins are not forgiven!

4. We would not have new life in Christ

Christianity is all about new life - a change from the old to the new. But this new life is dependent on the resurrection.

"Praise be to the God and Father of our Lord Jesus Christ! In his great mercy he has given us new birth into a living hope through the resurrection of Jesus Christ from the dead." **(1 Peter 1:3)**

"We were therefore buried with him through baptism into death in order that, just as Christ was raised from the dead through the glory of the Father, we too may live a new life." **(Romans 6:4)**

5. We would not have hope of Eternal Life

If He hadn't come back to life, we would have no hope at all. No hope that God is able to do all things. No hope of heaven. No hope of seeing our faithful loved ones again. Without hope, our lives would be terrible. We would be living for today only. If Jesus didn't resurrect from the dead, then He was defeated by death, and therefore, death defeats us too.

The good news is this....Jesus DID resurrect from the dead. He is who He says He is. In Him we have faith, and hope, and forgiveness of sins, and new life. In Him we are resurrected from the dead and have the promise of eternal life with Him.

And here is even more good news...... if Jesus resurrected from the dead, then He's still alive! He is :

"seated at the right hand of the throne of the Majesty in heaven" (Hebrews 8:1)

He is our mediator. He is our High Priest. He will never leave us or forsake us, and He is coming back some day to gather His church.

If the chief priests would have been right and Jesus was a fake, then the Jesus movement would have died out long ago. But they were wrong, and the one who was victorious, not just over them, but over death itself, was Jesus. When He actually came back to life, that was the knock out blow for all the non believers, especially the chief priests and the Pharisees.

FINAL SCORE:

JESUS 3 -   CHIEF PRIESTS 0

"I am the resurrection and the life. The one who believes in me will live, even though they die." (John 11:25)

CHAPTER 19

Will A Doomsday Meteor Destroy The World?

I saw a huge meteor fall only twice in my life. Once, years ago, around sunset, a huge fireball appeared to fall vertically, straight down to the horizon. Another time when I was on my deck, in broad daylight, I saw something bright, trailing straight across the sky. It looked like a jet at first, but as it got closer, I could clearly see it was a ball of flame with a smokey tail. I could even hear it! A loud swishing, burning sound clearly could be heard as it moved by. It never appeared to fall, but continued horizontally until it went out of sight, from one end of the sky to the other. I had never seen anything like it before or since.

I've heard that a lot of these burning objects may be space debris or small meteors that burn up. And occasionally on the news, there are reports of meteors actually hitting the ground, like the recent large one in Russia that struck the ground earlier this year. It sent a shock wave that broke hundreds of windows nearby! Fortunately, no one was killed.

If you search the internet, you'll find several claims of people recovering a small meteorite, or even some who claim to be hit by one. Who knows how many of these stories are true. I know one thing, if you are ever hit and killed by a meteor, your appointed time on this earth is definitely up! I mean, what are the odds of that!

So, the question is, will a huge doomsday meteor someday cause the total destruction of the world? There are books about it. There are movies about it. There are TV shows about it. Scientists are scheming how to destroy such an object, or knock it off course, with lasers or rockets or weapons of some sort.

When you think about it, a meteor would have to be enormous to actually break up the earth and destroy it. Actually, a meteor is relatively small, where an asteroid is a much larger object. Could an asteroid demolish the earth? Probably not. It would take something like the size of another planet to do it. But there isn't anything that big randomly hurling through space. (I think)

Even if the earth itself isn't destroyed in some huge collision, could a large meteor, or an asteroid, at least wipe out all life on earth? Maybe so (as I look over my shoulder). Seriously though, it's amazing to think how God, in His magnificent design of the universe, has created such a life-sustaining planet as earth.

Just the idea that we live on a sphere is amazing. How can we walk upright, on top of the globe as well as on the bottom? Yes I know, gravity. But gravity is still to this day unexplainable! Even Einstein couldn't completely figure it out. And scientists of today still cannot fully explain what causes gravity. We know what it is and what it does, but the question remains....what causes gravity to work? What is its source? No one can completely explain it. That's why I believe gravity is a God thing.

Gravity is one of those mysterious areas that we'll never have an answer for. It's like trying to figure out where the universe ends, and if there is an end to the universe, what's on the other side? All these mysteries just point to a Creator God.

One reason why a killer meteor or asteroid has not yet wiped out life is because God has designed protective measures and put them in place. One such example is the earth's atmosphere. It burns up meteors before they hit the ground (usually, hmmm).

Some scientists claim that Jupiter is a protective planet, and that its huge size and gravitational force is able to draw meteors away from the earth. If you believe in a Creator God, this is just another demonstration of His amazing foresight in protecting our planet.

But if God created the earth, and has protected it, He could surely wipe out life if He desired to do so. He almost did it once - by the great flood. Because of man's unrighteousness, He had enough of man's sin and rebellion, and destroyed almost everybody with a flood. Only Noah and his family, eight in all, were found to be righteous, and survived. At least we know that God won't use a flood again to wipe us all out. He promised that.

"I establish my covenant with you: Never again will all life be destroyed by the waters of a flood; never again will there be a flood to destroy the earth." **(Genesis 9:11)**

So, what does the Bible say about the end times then? How does the Bible say the world will end? Well, it looks like a fiery ending! (Yikes!)

"But the day of the Lord will come like a thief. The heavens will disappear with a roar; the elements will be destroyed by fire, and the earth and everything done in it will be laid bare. Since everything will be destroyed in this way, what kind of people ought you to be? You ought to live holy and godly lives as you look forward to the day of God and speed its coming. That day will bring about the destruction of the heavens by

fire, and the elements will melt in the heat." (2 Peter 3:10-12)

If God is in control and is planning a Final Day, a Judgment Day, then obviously the earth, or at least all life on earth, will someday be obliterated, but only when God decides the timing is right. In other words, if God wanted to (maybe when He's had enough of sinful man), He could hurl a flaming giant asteroid, or something like it, right at us! If so, there's nothing we can do to stop it. After all, He's used fire before - on the sin-ridden cities of Sodom and Gomorrah.

"Then the Lord rained down fire and burning sulfur from the sky on Sodom and Gomorrah. He utterly destroyed them, along with the other cities and villages of the plain, wiping out all the people and every bit of vegetation." (Genesis 19:24-25)

So.....will a doomsday meteor trigger the end of the world? Maybe!! And if so, what shall we do to prepare ourselves for a doomsday meteor, asteroid, or whatever else might wipe us out? Simple....the best way you can prepare for the end of the world is to make sure you are right with God! Then you can stop worrying about it.

CHAPTER 20

Paranormal Activity – Jesus Levitates!

Jesus was involved in paranormal activities. Of course! Because He was and is 'paranormal'. Paranormal means not scientifically explainable. In other words, definitely NOT Normal. That's because when Jesus came to earth, He was in very nature God, taking on the appearance of a man (Philippians 2:6-8).

Jesus performed a ton of miracles. Miracles are events that defy the laws of nature and science. Jesus healed the sick, made the blind see, made the deaf hear, walked on water, calmed the sea, fed the hungry, healed the crippled, drove out demons, and even raised the dead back to life! Whoa! And that's just a sampling. Besides specific miracles that are recorded in the New Testament, with specific people, the Bible also talks about general miracles that Jesus did - whole groups of people with various issues.]

"Jesus saw the huge crowd as he stepped from the boat, and he had compassion on them and healed their sick." (Matthew 14:14)

"A vast crowd brought to him people who were lame, blind, crippled, those who couldn't speak, and many others. They laid them before Jesus, and he healed them all." (Matthew 15:30)

"Large crowds followed him there, and he healed their sick." (Matthew 19:2)

Who knows how many were healed. Hundreds, perhaps thousands over the period of His ministry. The Gospel of John details many miracles by Jesus, however, not every miracle is recorded.

"Jesus did many other things as well. If every one of them were written down, I suppose that even the whole world would not have room for the books that would be written." (John 21:25)

Some of the paranormal activities Jesus was involved in were not just Him performing miracles, but events in His life. For instance, His birth was paranormal. He was born of a virgin! Impossible you say? According to the laws of nature, yes. But, the Creator God invented nature and has sovereignty over it. He can alter it any way He wants to, at any time He wants to. And how about at the baptism of Jesus? The Holy Spirit descends like a dove, settling on Him, and God speaks audibly from Heaven! (Matthew 3:16-17) Not normal! Supernatural!

The 'transfiguration' of Jesus was another incredible paranormal event.

There he was transfigured before them. His face shone like the sun, and his clothes became as white as the light. Just then there appeared before them Moses and Elijah, talking with Jesus. Peter said to Jesus, "Lord, it is good for us to be here. If you wish, I will put up three shelters—one for you, one for Moses and one for Elijah." While he was still speaking, a bright cloud covered them, and a voice from the cloud said, "This is my Son, whom I love; with him I am well pleased. Listen to him!" (Matthew 17:2-5)

Of all the paranormal events Jesus was involved in, the most astounding, far reaching, eternally significant one is His resurrection from the dead! Wow! Because He resurrected, Jesus defeats death itself, and if we are in Christ, we defeat death also. We will resurrect from the dead, and have eternal life with Him, in Heaven.

"And if the Spirit of him who raised Jesus from the dead is living in you, he who raised Christ from the dead will also give life to your mortal bodies because of his Spirit who lives in you." (Romans 8:11)

After Jesus resurrected from the dead, He walked on earth for 40 days, and was seen by many, including 500 at one time (1 Corinthians 15:6). And then something incredible happened. After giving some final instructions to His disciples, He levitated right before their eyes. That's right! Paranormal activity again! To levitate means to rise or float in the air, in defiance of the physical laws of gravity. Jesus, in bodily form, began floating upward, higher and higher, until He reached the clouds and beyond, and then out of sight.

"After saying this, he was taken up into a cloud while they were watching, and they could no longer see him." (Acts 1:9)

Can you imagine what the disciples were seeing and thinking? They were trying to see Him as long as they could, for as far as they could, but eventually He was too far away. It's hard to say how long they would have stared into the sky. Fortunately, two angels interrupted their straining. The angels told them that Jesus ascended into the spiritual realm - Heaven.

As they strained to see him rising into heaven, two white-robed men suddenly stood among them. "Men of Galilee," they said, "why are you standing here staring into heaven? Jesus has been taken from you into heaven, but someday he will return from heaven in the same way you saw him go!" (Acts 1:10-11)

Since Jesus was raised from the dead, He is alive! Death no longer has dominion over Him, or over us for that matter. And since Jesus ascended into Heaven, He is going to come back to get us - His church. He promised that.

"Don't be troubled. You trust God, now trust in me. There are many rooms in my Father's home, and I am going to prepare a place for you. If this were not so, I would tell you plainly. When everything is ready, I will come and get you, so that you will always be with me where I am." (NLT, John 14:1-4)

His return will be the "grand finale" - "the coup de grace". No one knows when He will come back. But one thing is for sure, He will! And when He does, He will judge the living and the dead, and there will be some amazing paranormal activity, like that which has never been seen. So.... BE READY!

"No one knows about that day or hour, not even the angels in heaven, nor the Son, but only the Father. Be on guard! Be alert! You do not know when that time will come." (NIV, Mark 13:32-33)

CHAPTER 21

How Jesus Could Have Avoided The Cross!

If you wanted to torture someone to death in the cruelest, most horrifying way - in a way that would not only be a long, drawn out, painful death, but also a completely humiliating one - it would be by crucifixion - no one survives it. It's a death penalty.

Yes, Jesus was tortured to death. But here is what's of utmost importance....Jesus could have escaped the cross if He wanted to! One of the fundamental truths of Christianity is this: Jesus was crucified only because He allowed it to happen!

Although Jesus died on the cross, taking on the role of a sinner, He was totally innocent. He never sinned. He never broke the laws. He never deserved to be put to death. The truth is, His death on the cross was His intention! It was His mission, and nothing was going to stop Him. He went to the cross willingly.

"The reason my Father loves me is that I lay down my life—only to take it up again. No one takes it from me, but I lay it down of my own accord. I have authority to lay it down and authority to take it up again. This command I received from my Father." (John 10:17-18)

What He was saying is that no one is capable of taking His life by force. There is no power, no authority, no force that is strong enough. Instead, Jesus as the Lamb of God, gave His life - offered His life as the sacrifice for our sins.

He is the only sacrificial offering that satisfies the wrath of God for our sins. Jesus made clear His ultimate intention when He said:

"I am the good shepherd. The good shepherd lays down his life for the sheep." (John 10:11)

Jesus could have escaped the cross if He had wanted to, at any time, at any place. But let's just look at His arrest scene alone. There we find no less than three chances where Jesus could have avoided being captured, but He chose not to.

Avoiding Arrest - Option #1 (Fight)

The first instance involves Peter. If you remember, Judas had arranged to turn Jesus in for thirty pieces of silver. Judas came to the garden where Jesus had been praying, guiding a detachment of soldiers. When Jesus' followers saw what was going to happen, they said, "Lord, should we strike with our swords?" They were armed, ready to fight and defend Jesus. At that moment, Peter drew his sword and struck the high priest's servant, cutting off his right ear.

However, Jesus said, "No more of this!" Jesus even reacted to Peter's attack by touching the man's ear and healing him, perfectly restoring the man's ear. Jesus commanded Peter:

"Put your sword away! Shall I not drink the cup the Father has given me?" (John 18:11)

Later on, Jesus explains to Pilate:

"My kingdom is not of this world. If it were, my servants would fight to prevent my arrest by the Jewish leaders. But now my kingdom is from another place." (John 18:36)

So you see, Jesus could have had His disciples fight to defend Him from arrest, but He chose not to. Instead of escaping arrest, He avoided confrontation, having His followers put their swords away.

Avoiding Arrest - Option #2 (Supernatural Power)

The second instance where Jesus could have easily avoided being captured and arrested occurred right after He identified Himself to the mob. This time, in my view, it involved a miracle - an amazing demonstration of supernatural power. Jesus, knowing all that was going to happen to Him, went out and asked them:

"Who is it you want?" "Jesus of Nazareth," they replied. "I am He," Jesus said. When Jesus said, "I am He," they drew back and fell to the ground!" (John 18:4-6)

It seems that when Jesus identified Himself using the Holy Name of God, "I Am", there was power in those words.

Some people say that the soldiers were simply startled and stumbled backward. On the other hand, I visualize what happened as some sort of invisible, supernatural shock wave. When He says, 'I Am He', not only revealing Himself as the one they are looking for but as God in the flesh, they are knocked down. He could have not just knocked them down, but wiped them out!

I'm reminded of this verse:

"that at the name of Jesus every knee should bow, in heaven and on earth and under the earth, and every tongue acknowledge that Jesus Christ is Lord, to the glory of God the Father." (Philippians 2:10-11).

Avoiding Arrest- Option #3 (Angels)

There's a third way Jesus could have easily avoided being captured and arrested. In the midst of the arrest scene, right after Peter cuts off the servant's ear, Jesus said to Peter, "Put your sword back in its place, for all who draw the sword will die by the sword." Then Jesus made an amazing statement - a revealing statement.

"Don't you realize that I could ask my Father for thousands of angels to protect us, and he would send them instantly?" (Matthew 26:53 NLT)

At any instant, at any time, Jesus could have invoked the powers of Heaven to intervene for Him, immediately - on the spot! Instead, He doesn't call on those resources which are right at His fingertips, but allows the arrest to happen.

So, just in the context of the arrest scene alone, we find no less than three instances where Jesus could have easily resisted arrest. First, He could have ordered His followers to draw their weapons and fight off the mob. Second, He could have used supernatural power to wipe out the mob. Third, He could have called thousands of angels to rescue Him and His followers from the mob.

Instead, He chooses not to interfere, or have his followers interfere, with the arrest. That's because He knows the timing is right and His arrest will surely lead to the unfolding of the plan of the cross - the unfolding of the plan that was conceived before the creation of the world. He knows the time is at hand for this to happen - the arrest which will lead to His crucifixion, and ultimately, to Him offering Himself as the Lamb of God who takes away the sins of the world.

Why?

So, the question is why? If Jesus could be crucified only if He allowed it to happen, why was He so compelled to carry it out? Why would Jesus willfully die on the cross for our sins?

You see, because of our sins, each one of us is given a death penalty.

"The wages of sin is death..." (Romans 6:23)

If our sin earns us the death penalty, why would Jesus pay the penalty of death for us? What is the motivation? The answer?.... Love!

Jesus understood this when He said:

"Greater love has no one than this: to lay down one's life for one's friends." (John 15:13)

God Himself was motivated by love.

"For God so loved the world that he gave his one and only Son, that whoever believes in him shall not perish but have eternal life." (John 3:16)

You see, the bottom line is God's love for us.

"...because of his great love for us, God, who is rich in mercy, made us alive with Christ even when we were dead in transgressions—it is by grace you have been saved." (Ephesians 2:4-5)

Yes, Jesus was tortured to death on a cross. But only because He allowed it to happen! And all because He loves you, and wants you to become one of His.

"For the wages of sin is death, but the gift of God is eternal life in Christ Jesus our Lord." (Romans 6:23)

CHAPTER 22

How Ezekiel Opened My Eyes To The Big Picture

A few of us met at my office (the local Panera's) recently for a morning Bible study on the book of Ezekiel. It took us months to go through it verse by verse. We met once a week, 7:30 each Monday morning, and did about a chapter each time. First we would talk a bit, sip on some coffee, and more often than not, I would jokingly ask who's bright idea was it to study this book. That's because Ezekiel is kind of intimidating to study because of it's imagery and symbolism, and a lot of people just either skim through it or simply stay away from it.

In case you didn't know, Ezekiel is one of the Old Testament books of the Bible, named after the writer, who was one of the prophets of God. Ezekiel lived around 600BC. He was among those Jews who were brought into captivity in Babylon. It was a time when the nation of Israel, God's chosen people, had become disobedient, corrupt, arrogant, and were worshiping idols instead of worshiping God. This had been going on for a long time and God became so fed up with their disobedience that He decided to wipe most of them out and destroy all their idols.

God began giving Ezekiel visions, calling him to become a prophet. The first vision was spectacular, one that no doubt caught his attention. It's the famous vision of spinning wheels inside of wheels. Essentially what it meant was the God was going to remove Himself from His presence in Jerusalem.

Then chapter after chapter Ezekiel gives warning after warning, prophesying about the coming destruction of Jerusalem. This destruction would be by God's own hand of judgment, using the Babylonians as his vehicle. At first God told Ezekiel he would be unable to speak, so he acted out various predictions. For example, he would lay on his side in the direction of Jerusalem, or build models of the coming destruction of Jerusalem. Then, after the destruction of Jerusalem, he was allowed to speak and often against other nations such as Egypt and Tyre, who were holdouts against Babylon, the nation God wanted to use as His agent of judgment.

The book of Ezekiel ends with a glorious vision of the new Jerusalem in all its splendor. This could mean, symbolically, the coming New Testament church of Jesus Christ, or even the eternal Holy City of heaven talked about in Revelation. Regardless, it is a vision of restoration and promise.

As we went through the book, occasionally I would try to summarize what we had been studying so far. At first, I summarized the book, from a big picture view, like this:

Disobedience.....Punishment

But when we got toward the end of our study on the book of Ezekiel, I summarized it this way:

Disobedience.....Punishment.....Restoration

However, what I began to realize was that the big picture view of Ezekiel is really this:

Disobedience.....Purification.....Restoration

It began to make sense that, because of disobedience, God needed to punish the nation of Israel for worshiping other gods. He would destroy Jerusalem and many of the people there. Although their punishment was justified, it was actually part of a purification process. You see, God didn't totally annihilate His people and wipe them out completely. There was a remnant left - a remnant of the faithful. Because of this purification of Israel, God's chosen nation could be restored from the remnant.

What is even more amazing, is that this principle of Ezekiel, "Disobedience-Purification-Restoration", is the underlying principle of most of the other prophets as well. Not only that, it is the underlying big picture concept of the entire Bible as a whole. Think of it this way....sin came into the world through Adam and Eve (Disobedience). Forgiveness of sin was needed for mankind to be reconciled to God (Purification). This purification is only found through the sacrifice of the Lamb of God, Jesus, who offered to take the punishment we deserve. And finally, by His grace, the relationship between God and His people could be reconciled. (Restoration).

Disobedience.....Purification.....Restoration

What really is amazing is that this principle of Ezekiel, "Disobedience-Purification-Restoration", actually applies not only to the big picture of the Bible, but it applies to the big picture of our own individual lives as Christians!

You see, because of sin (Disobedience) we become separated from God. We then need a Savior, Jesus, who came to die for our sins (Purification) to take our punishment, so we can be reborn into a new creation, reconciled into a loving relationship with Him (Restoration).

Thank you, Ezekiel, because from a sometimes intimidating, confusing book, you have clearly brought out a simple, but powerful, principle. It's the big picture of the Gospel message.

Disobedience.....Purification.....Restoration

Thank you Ezekiel. Thank you Lord.

CHAPTER 23

Life Is Better When You're Not In A Hurry

It's easy to get caught up in this fast paced society we live in. After all, everything is geared for speed. Our cars are fast, our food is fast, our internet is fast (or sometimes fast).

However, I recently was reminded that life is better when you're not in a hurry. It occurred to me when I was driving down the road one morning on my way to the beach, in the off season. I'm fortunate to live near the beach, and I try to get there as often as I can, even if it's to get a glimpse of the ocean, just to see what's going on.

So I was driving along, not in any real hurry because it was my day off. And as an experiment, I decided to drive the speed limit, 50mph. Then I began to realize something. It was kind of nice! I was starting to enjoy just cruising along at an easy pace, with no appointment to rush to, and no particular place to go except the beach. It was then that I realized that life is so much better when you're not in a hurry all the time.

I felt like I had time to just look at the scenery, the sky, and trees and the various colors around me as I slowly sailed down the highway. That is, until I was broken out of my trance by a glance in the rear view mirror. There was a line of about 10 cars behind me! So much for driving in a daze. I had to get going, so I wound her up to 59mph.

No more relaxing now. I had to get those guys off my bumper. I slowly pulled away, only to find that after about 2 or 3 miles I came upon a car going really slow. He was going 35 in a 50! I couldn't believe it. Pokey!!! (A pokey is defined as someone who is driving UNDER the speed limit). You need to realize that I was on a single lane road with double lines the whole way - no passing for miles.

Finally, I was able to get around the slow poke when the 2 lane road eventually went into 4 lanes. For a long while I was pulling away, when I noticed an upcoming traffic light turning red. And as usual, I was the first one at the light. (This happens all the time to me because I have this "first one at the red light" curse. It's hereditary.)

Guess who pulled up right behind me. The pokey!! Then I realized I was the hare, and he was the tortoise. Did you ever notice that when you pass someone and get a real good jump on them, that before long, a couple of traffic lights or stop signs later will nullify your lead and you will find them right behind you anyway? It's like the tortoise and the hare story. So maybe the tortoise has the right idea.

So why are we always too busy? Always in a hurry? Always stressed? Welcome to the United States of America! That's who we are. I wonder if we are the only country in the world so hyper. When I visited Africa a couple of years ago, the pace is totally different - slower. It was kind of nice! What everyone seems to lack here in the U.S. is slow-down time - solitude time - quiet time.

I need to remind myself to slow down. That's why I have what's sort of my motto on the back window of my truck. Right behind the driver's seat, I have some vinyl lettering that says, **"Matthew 13:1 NKJV"**. What that passage says is this:

On the same day, Jesus went out of the house and sat by the sea."

If Jesus took time to get away and sit by the sea side, it's good enough for me. I love this passage so much that it's now sort of become my motto - my inspirational verse. Time on the beach is my perfect solitude time. I have a four wheel drive truck with a surf fishing permit that allows me to drive on the beach in certain access areas 24/7, year round. I love the beach. There's just something special about the sight of the vast sea, the rhythm of the waves, and the smell of the sea air.

I've often wondered....what motivated Jesus to leave the house and sit by the sea side? But if you look at the events that lead up to it, in Matthew chapter 12, you can see why. Things were intense. He was being challenged by the Pharisees, was teaching, was performing miracles, and even had his mother and brothers waiting to confront Him. After all that, I'm sure He wanted time to get away, time to think, time to pray, and have some solitude time.

The moral of the story.......in your busy day-to-day life, take time to take a breather, even if for just a moment. Try to find a little solitude. Remind yourself about the image of Jesus sitting by the sea. Place yourself there, and inhale a deep breath of the fresh sea air through your schnozzola (that means your nose).

And work on some things that help you not be in a hurry - like getting up a little earlier, like leaving you home a little early, like scheduling in some quiet time. Even try to drive the speed limit once in a while. Just don't be a pokey.

And remember, life is better when you're not in a hurry!

CHAPTER 24

How Nik Wallenda's Tightrope Walk Glorified God

On Sunday, June 23, 2013, Nik Wallenda walked across the Grand Canyon on a tightrope. Actually, it was a metal cable, a mere 2 inches in diameter, stretched 1400 feet from side to side, and 1500 feet above the canyon floor. He used no net and no safety harness! He made it across in just under 23 minutes. It was broadcast live around the world by the Discovery Channel.

Can you imagine! Remember, this cable is not 2 inches wide, it is 2 inches in diameter. No way could I even balance myself on such a cable, let alone walk on it. How do you stand on a wire? Then, to factor in the strong wind rising from the canyon, the extremely long cable swaying and vibrating, and the risk of falling! Wow! It's crazy.

Why would someone do this? Here's how Nik explains it, "My family has done this for seven generations and 200 years, and I'm carrying on a legacy. This is something I've done since I was 2 years old, and it truly is my passion." Now that starts to make sense to me. It's about family, tradition, and mainly, passion. Crazy as far as I'm concerned, but that's who he is - a Wallenda - brought up and groomed to do such things. The 34 year old is a member of the famous "Flying Wallendas" - a family of high wire acrobats. He started tight rope walking when he was 2. He is highly skilled, highly trained, highly experienced, and extremely qualified.

Some call him a daredevil. But from what I'm gathering, although he surely is daring, he is far from a devil. Rather, Nik is strong in his Christian faith. And my take away is that this whole tight wire walk across the Grand Canyon actually glorified God. Why do I say that? Because, thanks to a live microphone that was attached to him, we could hear him praying the entire way across the canyon. It glorified God because of his acknowledgement of God, of Jesus, of creation, of his trust, of his peace. He relied on God to help him. It's obvious that Nik Wallenda is someone who strongly believes in God, and is not afraid to publicly proclaim it. And it's refreshing and inspiring.

Below is a sampling of his actual remarks as he made his long and dangerous walk:

"Thank You Jesus"

"Praise You Jesus"

"Lord, help this cable to calm down."

"Praise You God"

"How I love you, Jesus"

"You're my King, my Savior, You're my Protector, my Shield, my Strength"

"Yes Jesus, yes Jesus, yes Jesus"

"God, You're so good, calm those winds in the name of Jesus"

"Help me to relax Lord, help me to calm down and relax"

"The enemy has no hold on me"

"The peace that passes all understanding"

"Lord, shine Glory upon Your name somehow Lord"

"Lord, I give You the Glory on this"

"Hallelujah"

"Lord, give me strength"

"Go away in the name of Jesus" (as he is squatting down, trying to calm vibrations in the cable)

"Thank you Lord, Thank you for calming that cable, Lord"

"God, calm those winds. You have authority over that, Lord. You have authority over that."

"In Jesus' name"

"You are the King of Kings"

"Thank you for this beautiful creation that You made"

"Lord, You are my everything"

"You are my all in all, my peace, my strength, my wisdom, my guidance"

"Glory to Your name"

Did Nik Wallenda believe that God would prevent him from falling? Not necessarily. He knew that was a possibility. Several family members died falling off the high wire, including his great-grandfather, Karl Wallenda, who died from a fall in 1978. It seemed, though, that with almost each inch he moved, he thanked the Lord for a successful step. I like that.

There's no doubt that his faith is real and sincere. "Faith plays a huge role in what I do," Wallenda said. "I believe God has opened many doors for me in my life and this is one of them. To inspire people around the World, let them know the impossible is not so impossible if you set your mind to it."

Some skeptics ask, if he fell to his death, what would he think of God then? Well, with someone who has such strong faith, Nik Wallenda would most likely say that his time was up, and that he is in a good place - in the presence of the Lord, the one he loves. "That's really where I get my peace," he said. "I have confidence that if something were to happen to me, I know where I'm going."

So, believe what you may about this man. As for me, I think his example of unashamed belief in God, his strong conviction and his public acknowledgement of his faith, is a lesson for all of us.

CHAPTER 25

How God Made Everything Out Of Nothing

One of the age old questions is this: "How did the universe begin?" It's another one of those mind-boggling topics. When man tries to explain how the universe began in a way that leaves out God, it's laughable. One such man-made God-less explanation is the Big Bang theory, which, if you ask me, is utterly stupid, unless God is in the picture.

So if God created the universe, a better question is this: "How did God create all things out of nothing?" I mean if nothing existed except the spiritual realm, how could a physical realm be created?

Consider this incredible verse that deals with creation:

"By faith we understand that the universe was formed at God's command, so that what is seen was not made out of what was visible." (Hebrews 11:3).

Wow! What a verse! There's the answer to how the universe began. It was formed by God's command, and it was formed out of nothing! Take it or leave it. As the verse above says, it takes faith that the universe was formed "at God's command". Faith is believing without even seeing, and without totally understanding, but simply trusting.

"By faith we understand that the universe was formed at God's command, so that what is seen was not made out of what was visible." (Hebrews 11:3).

The phrase in the above verse, "at God's command", implies that God has such creative force that all he had to do was speak the words, and the entire universe and everything in it was formed. If you look at all the creation verses in Genesis chapter one, they are commands. For example, God said:

"Let there be light, and there was light." (Genesis 1:3).

Now that is power! Do we need to figure out how God did it? No. Scripture states that "by faith we understand it". Settled. We just need to believe it. If the Bible says so, then it's truth.

Think about the last part of Hebrews 11:3 for a moment:

"...what is seen was not made out of what was visible." (Hebrews 11:3b)

That is an incredibly powerful statement. What it says is that everything in our physical existence was made out of nothing. And before the physical realm, only the invisible or spiritual realm existed. In other words, matter was not re-formed out of some previous existing materials but new matter was created, in a sense, out of thin air! "What is seen was not made out of what was visible." Settled. Either take that verse, the Bible for that matter, and believe it, or throw it out the window and go with the Big Bang theory. Your choice (you know where I stand).

And I know, we could, and maybe should (ha) stop here, but just for fun.....let's keep going. Because of the curiosity of our human minds which God gave us, we always try to comprehend these Bible truths. I'm no different. I just wonder – can the concept of God making something out of nothing be explained? How could this be done? It may be a crazy idea, and I may be wrong, but I've got a theory. (O boy here we go)

Here's my theory (from a non-scientist)........ If we break down everything that exists into its smallest components, there is a common building block. Whether we look at a piece of steel, a plant, an animal, a brick, a coffee mug, air or water – they all are made up of a combination of the same very basic elements. That, in itself, is incredible.

There are just over one hundred different elements that combine in various arrangements to make up everything in the physical dimension we exist in. For example, water is made up of 2 of the elements that are bonded together in a special combination: two Hydrogen atoms and one Oxygen atom, H_2O, form a water molecule.

Scientists have discovered that all atoms have the same three particles: electrons, protons and neutrons. The determining factor in identifying a specific element is the number of protons within the nucleus of an atom. These tiny particles (electrons, protons, and neutrons) are the foundation of all matter, and guess what? The electrons and protons are charged! In other words, they are energized! Each atom is like a miniature solar system held together by opposing electrical energy charges, with electrons orbiting the atom. Everything we see then, material or living, has as its fundamental building block - Energy!

One way to look at it is that energy is light, or light is energy. And in a sense, God is light, or at least created light. Could it be that everything that is in our physical realm is really some form of God-given invisible energy force, formatted and organized in such an orderly way as to create physical matter? God surely has the resources and ability to have done such a thing. God could have created matter out of thin air by arranging invisible energy in such a manner as to form everything from the smallest cell to the farthest star we can see in the universe! Awesome!

Nobel Prize winner Max Planck is quoted as saying this about the structure of matter – "As a man who has devoted his whole life to the most clear-headed science, to the study of matter, I can tell you as the result of my research about the atoms this much: There is no matter as such! All matter originates and exists only by virtue of a force which brings the particles of an atom to vibration and holds this most minute solar system of the atom together. We must assume behind this force the existence of a conscious and intelligent mind. This mind is the matrix of all matter. "

Regardless of how God created everything, one thing is for sure:

"By faith we understand that the universe was formed at God's command, so that what is seen was not made out of what was visible." (Hebrews 11:3).

OK, so maybe it's better not to try to figure things out like I have tried to do, and you can disregard my theory, that's fine. But don't disregard Hebrews 11:3.

"By faith we understand that the universe was formed at God's command, so that what is seen was not made out of what was visible." (Hebrews 11:3).

And perhaps the best thing to do is to simply take His word by faith, and praise Him with an attitude of wonder and amazement. Yes....that's a better way! As King Solomon once said:

"Much dreaming and many words are meaningless. Therefore, stand in awe of God" (Ecclesiastes 5:7).

When thinking of such things as creation, that's what we all should ultimately do..............

Stand in awe of God!

CHAPTER 26

How To Get Rid Of All The Evil In The World

A kidnapper in Cleveland, Ohio abducted 3 women and kept them locked up in his house for ten years. That guy is a monster. And we haven't even heard the half of it. Actually, I don't want to hear much more. I sure wouldn't want to be on that jury and listen to all that mess. They probably wouldn't let me on it anyway, because I'd say, "Guilty!", right off the bat!!!

With all that we see in the news lately, are things worse today than ever before? Maybe. But humans have always been really evil. Evil in the world is nothing new. It started with Cain and Able, children of Adam and Eve. Cain attacked his younger brother, Able, and killed him. Everything goes downhill from there. There was a time that evil became so predominant in the world that God decided to destroy the entire human race!

Then the Lord saw that the wickedness of man was great in the earth, and that every intent of the thoughts of his heart was only evil continually. And the Lord was sorry that He had made man on the earth, and He was grieved in His heart. So the Lord said, "I will destroy man whom I have created from the face of the earth, both man and beast, creeping thing and birds of the air, for I am sorry that I have made them." (Genesis 6:5-7 NKJV)

So, God sent the great flood that covered the earth. Fortunately, Noah was found righteous in the eyes of the Lord. He and his wife, his three sons and their wives (8 in all) were spared in the ark. Everyone else was wiped out. You know what that means? We are all descendants of Noah!

Unfortunately, thanks to Satan, the great deceiver and destroyer, it didn't take long for evil to creep back into the world. And so it goes. Even today.

What's really terrible is the fact that there is a lot more evil going on in this world than just what we hear on the news. Just in the US, according to the Center for Disease Control, there were 16,259 homicides in 2010! That's 45 murders every single day of the year, just in our country alone!!! And just think of all the other crimes going on. Then think of all the atrocities and crimes going on all over the world. Yes, this world is a mess. Seems that since the fall of man, the world always was a mess, is still a mess, and will always be a mess. There are, however, three ways that evil could be eradicated from the world.

(1) The first way to get rid of all the evil in the world is to wipe everything and everybody out! Well, that's unlikely to happen, unless God gets totally fed up with this world again. Don't rule that out though. He must be getting close!

(2) The second way is to convince people to be transformed and live new lives. In other words, convert everyone to real Christianity. By Christianity, I mean real, obedient Christ Followers. Well, we've been working on that, but it's a real battle.

(3) The third and sure way to get rid of all the evil in the world is for Jesus to come back, as He promised, and totally annihilate Satan and all evil. Since Satan is the root cause of all evil, then destroying Satan is the only way to

end evil. Satan and his followers will go to eternal damnation and Jesus and His followers will be take to eternal paradise. One thing for sure, when Jesus comes back, He's not coming back as a meek, humble servant.

Here's what the Apostle John saw in his vision of prophecy regarding the return of Jesus......

Now I saw heaven opened, and behold, a white horse. And He who sat on him was called Faithful and True, and in righteousness He judges and makes war. His eyes were like a flame of fire, and on His head were many crowns. He had a name written that no one knew except Himself. He was clothed with a robe dipped in blood, and His name is called The Word of God. And the armies in heaven, clothed in fine linen, white and clean, followed Him on white horses. Now out of His mouth goes a sharp sword, that with it He should strike the nations. And He Himself will rule them with a rod of iron. He Himself treads the winepress of the fierceness and wrath of Almighty God. And He has on His robe and on His thigh a name written: KING OF KINGS AND LORD OF LORDS. (Revelation 19:11-16 NKJV)

Now that's power! And authority! And victory! The book of Revelation goes on to describe how Satan is utterly defeated, and is ultimately tossed into the eternal lake of burning fire. So, if it takes Jesus coming back to end all evil in the world, I repeat the words of the Apostle John, near the end of the book of Revelation:

"Come, Lord Jesus!" (Revelation 22:20)

The sooner, the better.

CHAPTER 27

The Apostle Peter - Gunslinger?

OK - so I wanted to be sort of Biblically relevant with what's going on in our world. And right now, there's so much attention on guns and the right to have them, it made me wonder, how was it like when Jesus walked the earth, as far as personal weapons are concerned? Did the disciples carry personal weapons?

No doubt, it was a dangerous world back then. The Apostle Paul knew that well. Listen to his experiences:

"Five times I received from the Jews thirty-nine lashes. Three times I was beaten with rods, once I was stoned, three times I was shipwrecked, a night and a day I have spent in the deep. I have been on frequent journeys, in dangers from rivers, dangers from robbers, dangers from my countrymen, dangers from the Gentiles, dangers in the city, dangers in the wilderness, dangers on the sea, dangers among false brethren; I have been in labor and hardship, through many sleepless nights, in hunger and thirst, often without food, in cold and exposure." (2 Corinthians 11:24-27).

Certainly, it was a dangerous world. But not much has changed. It's a dangerous world today too. It makes you wonder though - what was it like to walk with Jesus and his disciples from town to town? Did they worry about robbers, muggers and thieves? Were they in dangerous places, around dangerous people? After all, the Bible does talk about Jesus being around sinners, tax-collectors, and such.

Later, Levi invited Jesus and his disciples to his home as dinner guests, along with many tax collectors and other disreputable sinners. (There were many people of this kind among Jesus' followers.)"   (Mark 2:15-17)

The more Jesus began to be known, the more His life was threatened.

"After these things Jesus was walking in Galilee, for He was unwilling to walk in Judea because the Jews were seeking to kill Him." (John 7:1)

Things seemed to get more dangerous for Jesus and the disciples as time went on.

"Then Jesus asked them, 'When I sent you out to preach the Good News and you did not have money, a traveler's bag, or an extra pair of sandals, did you need anything?' 'No,' they replied. 'But now,' He said, 'take your money and a traveler's bag. And if you don't have a sword, sell your cloak and buy one! 'Look, Lord,' they replied, 'we have two swords among us.' 'That's enough,' He said." (Luke 22:35,36,38).

Of course, no one could ever kill Jesus even if they wanted to, until it was the proper time - after His teachings were complete, after the disciples were trained, and after all prophecy was fulfilled.

"So they were seeking to seize Him; and no man laid his hand on Him, because His hour had not yet come." (John 7:30)

It seems in the later years, the Apostles were armed. Remember the famous incident when Jesus was arrested? The following is what happened when Judas the betrayer came with a group of Roman soldiers, looking for Jesus.

"'I am He,' Jesus said. (Judas, who betrayed Him, was standing with them.) As Jesus said 'I am He,' they all drew back and fell to the ground!'" (John 18:5-6)

I love the way Jesus momentarily demonstrated His power - He basically knocked them all to the ground by some supernatural power, just to show that He could never be taken by force. He could only be taken if He allowed it. (He died willfully on the cross for our sins). He could have wiped them all out if He wanted to.

The story of Jesus' arrest continues, and involves Peter drawing and using his sword! OK, it wasn't a gun - so Peter wasn't a gunslinger after all. However, Peter was a sword slinger!

When the other disciples saw what was about to happen, they exclaimed, "Lord, should we fight? We brought the swords!" (Luke 22:49)

"Then Simon Peter drew a sword and slashed off the right ear of Malchus, the high priest's slave." (John 18:10)

"But Jesus answered, 'No more of this!' And He touched the man's ear and healed him." (Luke 22:51)

You see, at that point, the time was right for Jesus to allow Himself to be arrested without a fight. After they took Him to Pilate, Jesus said:

"My kingdom is not of this world. If it were, my servants would fight to prevent my arrest by the Jews. But now my kingdom is from another place." (John 18:36)

It's important to note that the nature of Apostles' fighting changed after Jesus died, resurrected, ascended, and the church began. The Apostles were later empowered to fight, and would fight relentlessly, but no longer with physical swords. Instead, they would fight with spiritual ones. The Apostle Paul said:

"For though we live in the world, we do not wage war as the world does. The weapons we fight with are not the weapons of the world. On the contrary, they have divine power to demolish strongholds. We demolish arguments and every pretension that sets itself up against the knowledge of God, and we take captive every thought to make it obedient to Christ." (2 Corinthians 10:3-5)

So, what can we learn from all this? First, the Apostles were brave men. They were real men, not a bunch of wimps. They were courageous. They were Christ's disciples, but they were also His bodyguards and defenders. They were ready to fight for Jesus, if need be. They were men who were sold out, committed, devoted to Christ, and would lay down their lives for the cause.

Secondly, we need to stand strong in our own faith.

"Fight the good fight of faith." (1 Timothy 6:12).

"Be on your guard; stand firm in the faith; be men of courage; be strong." (1 Corinthians 16:13).

"Always be prepared to give an answer to everyone who asks you to give the reason for the hope that you have." (1 Peter 3:15).

One more thing - how does all this relate to our right to bear arms? I suppose it supports the basic right to be able to defend oneself. I'm not for taking away that right. If someone broke in my house trying to attack me or my family, I like the idea of having a gun available.

On the other side of the story, there should be a line drawn somewhere on what type of weapon a person should be allowed to have. Certainly, there's no need to keep a bazooka around the house. Or a nuclear bomb stored in the closet. We need to be reasonable. Does one really need a machine gun with a thousand rounds of ammo?

Better yet, it would be worthwhile to analyze the root cause of all these shootings. It's certainly not guns. I can't help but look at the TV shows and the movies that our culture thrives on. Just last week, I saw a commercial for the new upcoming Sylvester Stallone movie called, "Bullet To The Head." And have you seen how real the video games look today? And so many of them are filled with blood, killing and shooting.

Yes, our culture seems to thrive on violence for entertainment. Sad. Seems like our society is going down hill fast and following the course of the Romans. My brother, Tony, senses that. He sells bumper stickers that say, "We're Doomed." Our preacher, Mark, often mimics the words of the Apostle John in the book of Revelation, "Lord come quickly!"

CHAPTER 28

My Favorite Miracle

This is the tale of a collision between two processions. One of the processions was a funeral march coming out of the city of Nain, and one was a procession of Jesus and His followers approaching Nain.

"Soon afterward, Jesus went to a town called Nain, and his disciples and a large crowd went along with him." **(Luke 7:11)**

For some time, there had developed a multitude of people following Jesus wherever He went, as was the case here. And as it worked out, at the exact point in time when Jesus and His followers arrived at the gates of Nain, they met up with a funeral procession leaving the city.

Back then, with few exceptions, it was unclean for Jews to be buried inside the city walls. So they would take the corpse outside of the city gate to their designated burial ground. The dead were embalmed with spices, wrapped in cloth, and brought out on a bier, which was something like a stretcher. This practice of being wrapped in linen can be seen in the example of Lazarus as well as Jesus Himself.

"As he approached the town gate, a dead person was being carried out—the only son of his mother, and she was a widow. And a large crowd from the town was with her." **(Luke 7:12)**

Notice the two important points found in verse 12. First, it says that the dead person was an only son, and secondly, that the mother was a widow! In the culture of the day, when a husband died, the son would take care of his mom. But in this case, not only did the mother lose her husband, but now, she lost her only son. And with her only son dead, she was left alone, with no one to care for her.

Yes, two large crowds meet. Not for a dispute, not for a protest, not for a reunion, but for something unplanned, unforeseen, unimaginable - an astonishing miracle by Jesus. Jesus did a lot of miracles - most were to demonstrate His deity - His power - His authenticity - and to instill belief. However, the primary reason that Jesus performed this amazing miracle was not for any of those things, although all of them were sort of secondary spin-offs. The prime motivation for this miracle was strictly compassion.

"When the Lord saw her, his heart went out to her and he said, "Don't cry."" (Luke 7:13)

Of all the people assembled that day, notice who Jesus immediately focused on...the mother who was grieving. He wasn't focused on all the people. He wasn't even focused on the dead person. When Jesus saw the mom mourning, he saw her heart, and therefore, in response, His heart went out to her. And look at what Jesus says to the mom..... "don't cry". This says volumes about who Jesus is.

Moved by sympathy and compassion, Jesus not only comforts the mother, but He acts. What He does next is not the result of the mother's request, for she didn't request Him to do anything. And it's not the result of what the mother expected Him to do, because she didn't expect Him to do anything. For all we know, she didn't even know who He was! And I suppose that's why this is my favorite miracle of Jesus. It's a miracle strictly driven by compassion. Now Jesus did many miracles of compassion, but for me, this one demonstrates it the best.

This particular miracle was unprecedented by Jesus because it's the first time that Jesus raises someone from the dead. That's right, He raises the dead son back to life! Wow!

Then he went up and touched the bier they were carrying him on, and the bearers stood still. He said:

"Young man, I say to you, get up!" (Luke 7:14)

Jesus speaks directly to the dead young man, and commands him to come to life! What power and authority! And as with all of His miracles, they override the laws of nature, they are without failure, and they are totally complete. The young man not only sits up, but he immediately begins to talk! Jesus restores the son to his mother. Can you visualize the scene? Can you hear the mom's reaction? Can you imagine the crowd's response?

The dead man sat up and began to talk, and Jesus gave him back to his mother. They were all filled with awe and praised God. "A great prophet has appeared among us," they said. "God has come to help his people." This news about Jesus spread throughout Judea and the surrounding country. (Luke 7:15-17)

Talk about a feel-good miracle! And you can be sure of this next verse.

"Jesus Christ is the same yesterday and today and forever." (Hebrews 13:8)

That means that Jesus is just as compassionate today. That's the type of King we have. That's the type of God we have.

"Praise be to the God and Father of our Lord Jesus Christ, the Father of compassion and the God of all comfort, who comforts us in all our troubles, so that we can comfort those in any trouble with the comfort we ourselves receive from God." (2 Corinthians 1:3-4)

The lesson here is that God is a God of compassion, He's the Father of compassion, the originator of compassion, the source of compassion, and the example of compassion. We should therefore be compassionate also, and comfort those in any trouble with the comfort we ourselves receive from God. Let's put that into practice.

CHAPTER 29

Christian Zombies

Warning! - there may be Christian zombies in your midst! Even worse, you may be one yourself! What is a Christian zombie? Well, first of all, what is a zombie? It can be defined as "the body of a dead person given the semblance of life, by a supernatural force, usually for some evil purpose". In other words.....the walking dead!

So how does this apply to Christians? Well, as Christians, we are supposed to die to our 'old self', our 'sinful nature', our selfishness, our worldly ways. Christianity is all about new life - a new life of forgiveness and grace through Christ. So a Christian zombie is a Christian whose old self, the pre-Christian person you once were, the self-centered sinful-natured person you don't want to be, keeps trying to come back. And as a Christian, we are supposed to bury our old self, not bring it back! There's no better picture of this than Christian baptism, especially baptism by immersion.

"Or have you forgotten that when we were joined with Christ Jesus in baptism, we joined him in his death? For we died and were buried with Christ by baptism. And just as Christ was raised from the dead by the glorious power of the Father, now we also may live new lives." (Romans 6:3-4 NLT)

At our baptism, our old self dies and is buried, and we rise to walk in a new life, joined with Christ, united with Him. Over the years, I've seen dozens and dozens of people, hearing and understanding this concept for the first time, become so convicted that they are compelled to be baptized - many for the first time, and many re-baptized for the right reasons.

"For you were buried with Christ when you were baptized. And with him you were raised to new life because you trusted the mighty power of God, who raised Christ from the dead." (Colossians 2:12 NLT)

This new life is only possible because of the sacrifice of Jesus for our sins, and our belief and obedience to Him. New life = New start.

"This means that anyone who belongs to Christ has become a new person. The old life is gone; a new life has begun!" (2 Corinthians 5:17 NLT)

To illustrate further, when we decide to become a Christ follower, not only are we to undergo a spiritual death, burial, and resurrection, but we also go through a spiritual crucifixion! That's right, we crucify our old life style, our old self. You see, it's one thing to believe in the crucifixion of Jesus as simply a historical event, it's another thing to personally identify with it!

"We know that our old sinful selves were crucified with Christ so that sin might lose its power in our lives. We are no longer slaves to sin." (Romans 6:6 NLT)

So what does being crucified with Christ look like? It's a process of transformation from living for self into living righteously for God. It's becoming not just a "Christian", but a Christ follower - not just believing, but learning from Him and walking with Him, for life.

"Because of that cross, my interest in this world has been crucified, and the world's interest in me has also died." (Galatians 6:14b NLT)

So....if we crucified our old self, why would we want to resurrect it? Well, we don't!! - at least intentionally. It's when we slip up, yield to temptation, and fall back into our old ways, that our old self tries to return. That's why we need to be on guard. When we have a tendency to resurrect our old self, it makes you wonder if Satan has his hand in it. Remember the definition of a zombie?...."the body of a dead person given the semblance of life, by a supernatural force, usually for some evil purpose". I would bet that supernatural force is Satan tempting us, trying to convince us to resurrect that old self. But don't do it!

Some horror movies depict a grave yard scene where during a dark, rainy night, in the solitude of a lonely graveyard, a hand pops up from a grave, usually with some freakish music! Yikes! If you find this happening, spiritually, to you, stomp that hand back into the ground!

There are some ways to avoid becoming a Christian zombie. Below are five:

1. Stay Connected with the Word (the Scriptures)

"Do not conform to the pattern of this world, but be transformed by the renewing of your mind." (Romans 12:2a)

2. Stay Obedient to God's Commands

"If you keep my commands, you will remain in my love, just as I have kept my Father's commands and remain in his love." (John 15:10)

3. Stay focused on Jesus

"Since, then, you have been raised with Christ, set your hearts on things above, where Christ is, seated at the right hand of God. Set your minds on things above, not on earthly things. For you died, and your life is now hidden with Christ in God." (Colossians 3:1-2)

4. Stay in tune with the Spirit

"Those who belong to Christ Jesus have nailed the passions and desires of their sinful nature to his cross and crucified them there. Since we are living by the Spirit, let us follow the Spirit's leading in every part of our lives." (Galatians 5:24-25)

5. Stay in fellowship with other Believers.

"But if we walk in the light, as he is in the light, we have fellowship with one another, and the blood of Jesus, his Son, purifies us from all sin." (1 John 1:7)

Keep doing those 5 things, and you will never need to worry about becoming a Christian zombie!

CHAPTER 30

To Those Who Need Encouragement

Need a little encouragement for the new year? Don't feel alone. That's because every single person in the world, whoever was, whoever is, and whoever will be, needs encouragement. There's something about our human nature that requires it, that longs for it, that fuels us, that motivates us. For many, maybe even for you, the past year was not so good, and you are looking for a better year to come.

What is encouragement anyway? The dictionary definition would be to give support, confidence, or hope to someone - words that uplift, inspire, and motivate. Don't think you're beyond needing encouragement - that you are fine without it. Even Jesus needed to hear encouragement. Otherwise the Heavenly Father would not have spoken to him out loud 3 times in the New Testament. (1) At His baptism. (2) At the Transfiguration. (3) In the final days before His crucifixion.

(1) *As soon as Jesus was baptized, he went up out of the water. At that moment heaven was opened, and he saw the Spirit of God descending like a dove and alighting on him. And a voice from heaven said, "This is my Son, whom I love; with him I am well pleased."* (Matthew 3:16-17)

(2) *While he was still speaking, a bright cloud covered them, and a voice from the cloud said, "This is*

my Son, whom I love; with him I am well pleased. Listen to him!" (Matthew 17:5)

(3) *"Now my soul is troubled, and what shall I say? 'Father, save me from this hour'? No, it was for this very reason I came to this hour. Father, glorify your name!" Then a voice came from heaven, "I have glorified it, and will glorify it again." The crowd that was there and heard it said it had thundered; others said an angel had spoken to him.* (John 12:27-29)

MY TOP 5 ENCOURAGING VERSES

The Bible gives us wonderful truths to confidently place our faith in. There are many of them. You may have your own list, however, I decided to share my personal top five.

1. *".........Be strong and courageous. Do not be afraid; do not be discouraged, for the Lord your God will be with you wherever you go."* (Joshua 1:9)

2. *"For I know the plans I have for you," declares the Lord, "plans to prosper you and not to harm you, plans to give you hope and a future."* (Jeremiah 29:11)

3. *"And we know that in all things God works for the good of those who love him, who have been called according to his purpose."* (Romans 8:28)

4. *"And I am convinced that nothing can ever separate us from God's love. Neither death nor life, neither angels nor demons, neither our fears for today*

nor our worries about tomorrow—not even the powers of hell can separate us from God's love." (Romans 8:38)

5. *"And surely I am with you always, to the very end of the age."* (Matthew 28:20b)

May these verses be a blessing to you, and may you continually see God's hand at work in your life this coming new year. And remember to be an encourager yourself. Everyone around you needs it.

www.chipvickio.blogspot.com

Other books by Chip Vickio

"**Raise Up Your Praise!**
(How To Be Better At Praising God")

Available on Amazon.com

in paperback or Kindle.

www.ingramcontent.com/pod-product-compliance
Lightning Source LLC
Chambersburg PA
CBHW060322050426
42449CB00011B/2608